Memoirs

Of An

American Cowboy

A Collection of Real Life Stories Of Sherman Glen Hand

ARRANGED AND EDITED BY

STEVEN A. HAND

2nd Edition

iUniverse LLC
Bloomington

Memoirs Of An American Cowboy
A Collection of Real Life Stories Of Sherman Glen Hand

iUniverse books may be ordered through booksellers or by contacting:

iUniverse LLC
1663 Liberty Drive
Bloomington, IN 47403
www.iuniverse.com
1-800-Authors (1-800-288-4677)

ISBN: 978-0-5955-1886-9 (sc)
ISBN: 978-0-5956-2075-3 (ebk)

Printed in the United States of America

iUniverse rev. date: 07/09/2013

When I first saw these stories, I knew that we had to get them out for everyone to hear. Thank you Gramps for sharing your memories with us. Thank you Grandma for keeping watch over him and encouraging him to share. Thank you Michael for coming up with the title. And a special thank you to the whole family for providing pictures and filling me in with stories I didn't have. Here is to a century of life…

This new edition provides the final chapter of Grandpa's life, their last Christmas letter, and my thoughts of how he affected me. I call it simply, "The Final Chapter". I hope you enjoy this book as much as I enjoyed working with Gramps to get it published for him.

FOREWORD

In the early 1990's Sherman joined a story writing club in Rapid City. He needed topics for club meetings, so he began recording stories from his life. This book is a collection of those stories put in chronological order which developed into his life story. He was born in 1912 and is still playing pool and going for walks with his bride of over 70 years, in their retirement community well into their 90's. He's been to Hawaii, Canada, Mexico, Israel, Jordan, and most of the United States, most of which taking place since his 70th birthday. There are a lot of stories that aren't retold here, like dealing with a sheriff and an angry watermelon farmer, accidentally having lamb chops for supper, boxing matches in the Civilian Conservation Corps, stopping a fork fight over a campfire, and many others. But there's still time for a second edition!

These stories represent a small portion of the life and times of a man who impacted a lot of people's lives, from family, neighbors, life long friends, and recent acquaintances. He has left his mark, whether it was in the mountains of Wyoming, the prairies of Nebraska, or a stretch of highway in South Dakota, they would not be what they are now, in part, for who he is. He has seen the better part of a century when the United States was coming into its own internationally, brought electricity to the country, and met with two of its greatest battles on its own turf. He has seen man go to depths in the ocean never before possible and soared to heights far into our galaxy. He has seen the development of television and computers and global positioning satellites. What an ever growing world his generation has left for us and what broad shoulders on which we are able to stand.

This book contains his words and his memories so that we may share in his struggles and delight in his triumphs. May we, in some small way, experience a little part of the world as he saw it and as it has become.

Steven A. Hand

THE EARLY DAYS

MY MATERNAL GRANDFATHER, ANGUS Crinklaw, came from Scotland. His father and uncle lived fairly close to each other and went to Canada together. They homesteaded there. Our family decided to come into the United States. They came to Pennsylvania. That was my Grandpa's family.

Grandpa Crinklaw left home when he was 13 and went west. I suppose that he did a lot of odd jobs before he was rated as a cowboy. He was in Dodge City, Kansas when Billy the Kid was there and knew him. He probably came into the Black Hills freighting or because of the gold fever. Somehow, he became an Indian Scout for the Seventh Cavalry. He was in Montana when Custer was killed. He explored a lot of Wyoming and Montana.

He returned to South Dakota where he met and married Delia Caldwell in Spearfish. By this time, some of the trail herds had come north and some of the cowboys had started ranches. One of the ranches was called the Cross D. Most ranches took the name of their brand, as was in this case. It was one of the first in that part of Wyoming. Grandpa knew that country because he had been there. He took his new bride and went to work for the Cross D. Their first child was born there. When she was about one year old, they moved to a homestead in Montana near what later became a store and a post office called Ridge. The post office later moved about a half mile west. Grandpa was the first

1

to settle in that vicinity. They had nine other children, one of which was my mother.

My paternal grandfather and grandmother came from England, moved west through Nebraska, and homesteaded four miles south of Custer, Dakota Territory, in the same spot where later on the state would build a Tuberculosis Sanitarium. South Dakota didn't become a state until 1889. My father was born south of Custer and went to school in Custer. About 1905 his parents moved to Oakland, Oregon.

When Dad was seventeen, he and his older brother had gathered a few horses and decided to go to Montana to start a horse ranch. My dad was a real cowboy when a lot of Montana and Wyoming was wide open prairie with very few fences. Like a lot of the cattlemen, the homesteader was looked on as trash, but times were changing. People kept coming west and the homestead was a good way to get some land.

If you travel across Montana today in an automobile on a paved road, it seems very large. In 1906, when you were riding a horse, and there were just ruts for roads, no bridges across creeks, no fences, and no signs, it must have seemed to have no end. Dad and his brother kept going until they were about 25 miles west of my Grandpa Crinklaw's place. Dad's brother homesteaded a place there and they started their horse ranch. Dad went to work on another ranch to get some money for cows.

There was not much money, so the ranchers could only pay workers when they really needed help. These workers "rode the grub line". They just went to some ranch where they could help out for their room and board. They just did whatever needed to be done: they cut wood, mended fences, broke horses, carried water, or sometimes just visited.

There was not very much going on in the winter, and there were very few places for socializing. One of the ranchers would have a dance in his home just for fun or for some special occasion. People would come to these dances from as much as 50 miles away, especially if there were pretty girls around. I'm not really sure, but I'm guessing that my parents met at one of those socials.

Dad and Mom homesteaded about four miles from Grandpa Crinklaw. They built a little one room log house with a dirt roof. My sister was born there. Edna came prematurely on January 5th, 1910. She only weighed a little over two pounds. Grandpa kept her in cotton for about two months. Dad built a small frame house with two rooms. There was no electricity, no running water, and no bathroom. They used kerosene lamps for light. There were no telephones in that part of Montana. There were no automobiles so there were no oiled roads or bridges. Travel was by saddle horse, walking, or horse and buggy. From the time that we were babies, we had to be independent. To get water, they put a barrel on a horse drawn sled and went to a well about a quarter mile away. The well was next to a creek that was dry most of the year. When the creek was dry, they pulled water from the well by a bucket on a rope for 35 cows and five horses. The toilet was an outhouse in the

back with a Sears Roebuck catalog for toilet paper. We took our baths about once a week in the metal wash tub.

That is where my brother, Fred, and I were born. I was born June 30th, 1912. Fred was born on July 21st, 1914. My Grandfather Angus assisted in the birth of all three of us children.

I got my middle name from my father's middle name, Edgar Glen Hand. My first name came

Mom and Dad on their homestead

from a cowboy, who lived with the folks for a short time. His name was Sherman DeFord. He told my folks that if they named me Sherman, he would get me a pony. I got the name, but not the pony. When I got old enough to be told the story, I remembered Sherman DeFord's name because I never forgave him for not giving me the pony.

We raised a small garden, but we got much of our vegetables from Grandma and Grandpa. They had much better soil and raised a much larger garden. We had only wild or dried fruit. I only remember two times when we had fresh apples. The folks raised their own beef, chickens, and turkeys. The only fish we had were bull heads, which we caught in the dam.

The winter of 1912-13 was a real bad one. It started snowing in late October and didn't quit until the 20th of May. Everybody used sleds and a lot of four horse teams. It was long before automobiles, tractors, and four wheel drive trucks were frequent. Mom and Dad managed to tough it out that winter and things were a little better until the summer of 1919. That spring started out pretty good. Dad borrowed enough money to buy one hundred heifers. The summer turned dry and, of course, there was no hay. The winter was a repeat of 1912 and Dad lost all but thirty five head of his cows. He couldn't pay the bank. They took all he had left. He rode line again, looking after other people's stock on the open range until the spring of 1920.

Dad was gone a lot of the time. He worked for other ranchers riding line. There were no fences at that time. All cattle ran free. Our soil was made up of gumbo and bentonite which is an absorptive clay that was used as a filler in making paper. People would hire a rider to keep track of cattle and keep them from getting stuck in the mud of the creeks and dam. They also drove them back when they got too close to other cattle. In the fall there was a round-up. All the ranchers in an area got together and sorted out their own cattle. I guess that Mom got lonesome sometimes. We had a big horse. She put Fred in front of her on the horse and Edna and me behind her. We rode to Uncle Bob's and Aunt Janet's. Sometimes we went to Grandma's and Grandpa's. Old Barney was the horse we had then. I guess that is where I learned to love horses.

My uncle had a horse that was gentle. My aunt got along fine with him. They called him Red. Sometimes she would take us kids for a ride on him. My uncle just did not like that horse. He seldom used him. If that horse got a chance to leave my uncle afoot, he sure used to do it. It was just a case of "catch me if you can." Usually the horse won. Here would come Uncle Bob on foot and rather irritated.

I had always wanted to be a cowboy. When I was about five years old, my Aunt Janet had a mare which was struck by lightning. It had a colt. Aunt Janet gave the colt to us kids. When it was a year old, we started riding it. Dad had been riding on the open range just south of our place. He was taking care of the neighbors' cattle along with ours. He was home and was going out to check on the cattle. He was going to be gone for a just little while, so I got the colt and went with him. We had done what he needed to do and were headed back home. There was a lot of sage brush and sage hens. As we were riding along, a bunch of sage hens just exploded in front of us scaring our horses. I wasn't expecting it so I fell off and landed on the ground hard. I didn't know what happened until Dad was handing me to Mom.

There is a period between passing out and consciousness where you know what is going on but you can't do anything about it. You may do or say some crazy thing that has nothing to do with what other people are doing. I recovered from this first fall from a horse without any serious problem.

Dad had a few cows and worked to increase them. There was lots of open range in Wyoming and Montana to the south and east of our place. Several ranchers ran their cattle there in the summer time. Montana was a tough place to live. The saying used to be that it was tough on man and beast and hell on women.

Quite a few of Dad's horses were not so nice to handle. One horse in particular was real hard to catch. Dad took a long rope and staked him to a big old cottonwood log. He was real spooky. Being two lively boys, who needed to keep ourselves entertained, Fred and I went out a ways from the horse, threw our hats into the air, and yelled. That

Dad, me, and Uncle Bob

horse ran around that log and when he hit the end of the rope he broke the log in two. He ended up straddling the rope and then he really took off! He finally broke loose from the old log. When Dad got home, all he found was the long rope. Of course, Dad had to use his saddle horse to get the other horse back in the corral. Naturally, we hadn't seen what happened. I guess Dad figured that horse was wild enough to have done the damage without any help.

That spring, the folks decided to go out to Oregon to Grandpa Hand's. That was a disaster for everyone. We only stayed there over the winter. Fred got pneumonia and Dad was seriously ill with poison oak. Mom was not very well. She took us children and went back to Montana to Grandpa Crinklaw's. Dad stayed in Oregon and worked for the summer to get a little money. When he came home, they took me to Uncle Bob's to stay and Sis went to Belle Fourche to stay with Uncle Maurice and Aunt Mabel.

That summer my brother was six and I turned eight. Uncle Bob had a big shed and some corrals about two miles from the place. It was next to some open range where 30 or 40 head of horses were pastured. They would come into the shed to get out of the flies. By this time Fred and I were big enough so that we could take a horse and ride anywhere we wanted. There was another boy, ten years old, who wrangled horses for Uncle Bob. He stayed at my uncle's. The three of us got the idea that it would be fun to run some of the range horses into the chute, put saddles on them and let them buck. We did this three or four times. They sure did buck! We eventually saddled a big mare. She didn't seem very wild in the chute, but when we turned her out she made a couple of jumps and went under the shed. She hooked the horn of the saddle on barbed wire that was strung across to hold the shed together. She broke the cinch on the saddle. Oh! Oh! We were in trouble.

We took the saddle back and hid it in a dark corner of the barn. We put it behind some harness, hoping that no one would find it for awhile. Most ranchers know what goes on around them. Sure enough, Uncle Bob cornered us. He wanted to know what had happened to the cinch. We knew better than to tell him a story. We told him what we had been doing. He looked us in the eye and said that as long as we had told him the truth, he would not punish us that time. But he told us not to do it again because we might get hurt.

Kid's entertainment on the prairies between 1915 and 1922 was very different from today. We had no car, no telephone, no TV. There was no electricity. We used kerosene lamps and lanterns. The folks managed to get us one small wagon and a small doll buggy. We had two cats. We dressed one up and hauled it a few hundred miles in the doll buggy or wagon. The other one would go get a mouse or gopher and bring it to the one we hauled around. We didn't care much for our cat's meal but he seemed to like it.

If and when we went any place it was by walking mostly. Dad did have a wagon and team and saddle horses. If we went to Uncle Bob's, which was about two miles, we usually walked because it was more bother to get the horses. They were usually somewhere out in the pasture. If we went to Grandpa's, we often took the team and wagon. It was about five miles. Dad would get the team in for us.

Dad owned about six horses. We had a team of mares and two saddle horses. One horse he both worked and rode. He was our standby. He was old Barney. He taught us kids to ride. He had a lot of patience. He would stand perfectly still while we climbed on, regardless of how we did it or if there were a few more neighbor kids there. Mom could pile us three kids on him and go anyplace. She could also turn him loose with us and know that we might get a bruise or two or a smashed toe but no worse. He sure was a smart old horse. He would go just so far from the corral and then he would turn around and go back. He would never hurt us much, but he sure liked to step on our toes and hear us holler. I'm not sure where cuss words came from, but I'm sure old Barney helped invent some when Mom wasn't around. We rode from the time Mom could hold us on a horse, and we weren't very big when we were relegated to the back seat. Dad traded horses quite a bit and we were not very old when we had to try out a new horse. He had old Barney, a gray horse, and two mares that were not for sale or trade.

It was us kids' chore to milk the cows and keep the pigs out of the garden. Dad found a dog for Fred. She was a Collie and Airedale pup that we named Ginger. By spring Fred could send that pup into the pasture to get the milk cows. What a wonderful help. There was one old cow that would chase the dog. Ginger would get the cow to chasing her then Ginger would turn and head for the barn. The old cow went chasing after her and rest of the cows would come too.

We had a garden about half a mile from the house. We had a bunch of pigs that ran loose and of course, they liked our garden. There was one old sow that loved to get in our garden. She was the only one that Ginger couldn't keep out of it. One day that old sow was coming up along the fence close to the corral. It just happened that a pitch fork was leaning against the corral fence. I slipped out and grabbed the fork and sneaked behind that old sow. Ginger was right there with me. I jabbed that old sow in the back end and Ginger jumped up to grab an ear. She just made two nice little splits in that ear. From that time on, if that old sow started for the garden, all we had to do was holler, "Here, Ginger!" That old sow sure forgot about the garden!

That old sow had six baby pigs. Dad put her in a pen for a short time. In about three weeks, she had lost all but one. As dad was short on feed, he turned her out of the pen. Dad and I had just come from the corral, where he had milked the cow. For some reason, he had with him a bridle which had a heavy iron bit. That old sow was going across the yard with her little pig following.

Dad said, "Catch that little pig. She'll just lose it."

I said, "No! She'll get me!"

He said, "She won't pay any attention."

I slipped over and grabbed the little pig. It squealed and here came that old sow. I dropped the little pig. She ran over it. I dodged behind Dad. He had to hit that old sow on the nose with that heavy bit about three times before she had enough. We were lucky that Dad had that old bridle.

The folks had a log cabin, which had been their first house. At that time they were using it for storage. They had raised more potatoes than they could put in the cellar, so they put some in the cabin. It got so cold that they froze. By the time Dad got around to throwing them out, they had created quite a bit of alcohol. There were four pigs running loose. They came along and thought that those potatoes smelled pretty good. They started eating them, and evidently thought that was a good way to put on a party. I had never before or since, seen hogs act like that. They would squeal, stagger a ways, fall down, run into one another, and go around in circles. Finally they staggered together and I guess, decided that they had better sleep it off. Dad didn't know whether they would survive or not. It didn't seem to bother them after a couple of hours sleep.

When my brother got tired, he would go to sleep just anyplace he happened to be. It was my sister's and my job to keep track of him. He was about three years old and we were at our Uncle Bob's. We had been playing outside. There was a creek close by and it had some pretty deep holes. Sis and I got busy doing something and slipped up on keeping a close watch on Fred. One of the older folks, probably Mom, was checking up on us. No Fred! Of course, they worried about the creek. We searched and searched. Finally someone went into the bedroom.

That was the last place we would expect to find Fred, but there he was down behind the bed. He was sound asleep.

One day my father and I were working on some hog pens south of our house. The day was hot then about 10:00, a real big black cloud developed in the west. We knew that it was going to be pretty nasty because it was coming closer pretty fast. We were about a block from the house. Dad said that I had better scoot for the house, because it was really going to storm in about two minutes. He had to use those last two minutes, which was a mistake.

He had just started for the house when his hat blew off. Of course, he had to rescue his hat. The hat got caught in a fence, but it took long enough to rescue it, for the wind and rain to catch up to Dad.

When Dad got to the house he was soaking wet. Mom said, "I thought that you had sense enough to come in out of the rain."

He said, "Well, I'm not quite as smart as Sherman."

Just then, the hail knocked out the west window. Mom grabbed a quilt. Dad took it from her to hold up to the window. Mom got a washboard so Dad could use it and some chairs, or what ever, to hold the quilt up to the window. In the excitement, I looked out of the east window just in time to see our wagon and hayrack take off for our east corral. The wagon stopped when it hit the corral, but the hayrack took wings and blew over the corral. It was probably thirty feet in the air. It went end over end, and when it hit the ground it just exploded. It sure would have been kindling, if you could have found any pieces. I was scared and I was sure wondering what would happen next.

We were very lucky, because a storm like that can have very severe lightning. It sometimes kills cattle and horses, and even people once in a while. We did lose four hens from the hail. I don't remember what Dad did about the hayrack, but I remember about the washboard because the folks had a lot of fun talking about doing the laundry and sleeping in a wet bed.

There was no school near our home. My sister was a year and a half older than I. When she was old enough to go to school, she went to live with Grandpa and Grandma Crinklaw. There was a school about a mile and a half from their home. When I was six, Edna and I both went to Grandpa's to go to school. It was the first time that I had been away from home for any length of time. I got very homesick.

The year before, some of the men put up a single rope on a tree limb over a dry creek bed for a swing. It swung out over the creek bed and was six or eight feet from the creek bottom. They made the mistake of leaving the rope out all summer. It was slightly rotted by the time that school started. Since I was the youngest one in school, I was let out early. I had been swinging and doing just fine. I heard the bell to let the other kids out so I jumped on the swing for one more time. Bingo! The rope broke. I guess some of the kids saw me land. Anyway, when I came to, I was at Grandma's and Grandpa's and the folks came up. The next day we went back to school and there was a new swing. Oddly enough, there were no lawyers in that country. It wasn't so bad as long as the weather was warm and we were outside a lot. When it was cold and there were a couple of feet of snow on the ground, I wanted to go home.

That same fall, it started snowing in October. By the middle of November, we had about three feet of snow on the level and it was cold. Dad came up to see us and to get the mail. The post office was about two miles beyond Grandpa's. It was dark when he got to Grandpa's and darker when he came back from the post office. I was so homesick that I just couldn't let Dad go home without me. He finally gave in. He was riding one of his gentle horses that knew the way home. He put me up with him on the horse. For about the first two miles, we followed the old wagon road, then we had to go out across a big pasture of rolling prairie. There was a lot of snow on the ground, and it was as cloudy and dark as it can get. It was so dark that you couldn't see two feet in front of you. All we could hear was the crunch of the horse's feet on the snow. We were the only living things around. We got out into the middle of the pasture. Dad thought that he knew where he was going, but the horse wanted to go a different way. Finally Dad said, "Maybe you know where you are going because I sure don't." It was only about three miles across the pasture, but it seemed like we would never get there. Before long we wound up right at the gate close to the house. When Dad got off to open the gate he patted the horse and said, "You sure knew what you were doing. Thanks." No one could understand that feeling unless you had been on the prairie on a cold, cold, dark night in a foot and a half of snow. That was the end of school for me for that year.

The second year for me, Sis and I were at Grandpa's for about a month. We had gone home for some reason. While we were at home, the school house burned down. We had no more school for that year.

Mom really wanted us kids to get an education. Edna was the only one who had one year in school. A lot of discussion went on about what could be done.

That summer Dad was still riding for the ranchers and the neighbors put up our hay. That fall the folks decided to go to Grandpa Hand's in Oregon. Dad left first to get things sort of organized. Mom and us kids followed about two weeks later. It was our first sight of a train. We saw it at night and I will never forget the sight of that great big monster of an engine breathing fire. It was a coal burner, not a diesel.

Moving from a high dry climate to a lower wet one was a disaster. My uncle and dad sheared sheep and goats. There was a lot of poison oak and Dad was very susceptible to it. He swelled up so bad that he couldn't turn over by himself. Fred got pneumonia. The doctor stayed all night with Fred, not knowing if he was going to make it through the night. Both he and Dad finally improved enough so that Dad went back to work helping to build a big garage in Oakland. He got money enough to send Mom and us kids back to Grandpa's in Montana.

When we got back, Mom wasn't feeling very well. Dad got back about a month later. This must have been in the middle of August. They decided that they would have to take Mom to Hot Springs, South Dakota for an operation. I don't know how it was decided what to do with us kids. Uncle Maurice and Aunt Mabel, who lived in Belle Fourche, said that they would take Sis. Uncle Bob and Aunt Janet said that they would take me. Mom and Dad decided that they would take care of Fred. Dad packed up Mom and Fred and headed to Hot Springs. Dad looked up a man who had gone to school with him in Custer. That man had a ranch just south of Custer. The folks stayed there that winter.

That should have been the year of the third grade for me. I was going to ride a horse to school, because it was about three miles. Before I got started, the teacher decided that she was too far away from city folks, I guess. Anyway, she left and I spent the winter helping to feed cows. A young fellow and I would hitch four head of horses to a sled about daybreak, go about eight miles over the prairie and load up three loads of hay by pitch fork. We had to unload it to feed the cows there. Then we would get a load to take home and unload it for the cows there. Sometimes it would be after dark when we finished. It didn't make any difference how cold it was because we didn't have anyone to tell us what the wind chill was.

Mostly, I enjoyed that winter. On Saturday nights we would often hook up a team to the sled, put some hot, wrapped rocks on some hay in the sled. Then we got several good, heavy quilts and would take off for a dance or a party anywhere from within one to fifteen miles away. The horses were grain fed. The sleigh was light and the horses covered the ground—a whole eight miles an hour, I expect. It didn't seem like it took us very long to come or go. We got home about daylight.

Sometimes Sunday seemed rather long. We had a good, hot breakfast and took off to feed those darned hungry old cows. I really didn't get exposed to much formal English or to fractions in arithmetic that winter.

Being ten years old and having your family split up, even though you were getting good care, was hard. I was lonesome.

About that time, I got my wonderful pal and friend. He was the pup of Ginger, the dog Dad found for my brother, when my sister and I were staying with our grandparents and going to school. Our grandparents had been taking care of the dog for Fred. When she had puppies they thought that it was time for me to have a friend. So they gave me one of them. I called him Tippy. He had a white tip on his tail.

John Blaylock, the young man who was working for Uncle Bob, was a big pest. I liked him, but got mad at him once in a while. One time he ran around the house and acted like he had picked up my pup. He ran into an old building that had holes in the walls. He pretended to put the pup in one of the holes. I couldn't find my pup. John went back to the house to put on his overshoes. There was an old broken piece of a broom handle lying by the shed. I picked it up and was ready to clobber John right on the head. As usual, Aunt Janet was where she needed to be. She hollered or I might have been sorry because I didn't know how much damage I could do.

Like most country boys, since I was not going to school, I sure could be useful. My uncle had about 300 head of cows. He had two ranches. They were about six miles apart. He kept about 100 head of his cows on the home place. About the first of November, John and I started to haul hay to feed the other 200 head of cows. We used a sled and four head of horses. We would start before daylight and get home after dark. That pup never failed to see me off in the morning and be there to greet me when I returned at night. That pup grew into a real good ranch dog. He really liked working with cows. A fellow, who had some sheep, had seen what our dog would do. He offered us $50 for him. At that time that was like three months wages. It would have been like selling one of the family, so we kept Tippy.

We had no fresh fruit. Somebody went to Belle Fourche with a couple of sleds to get groceries. Aunt Janet had them get a bushel of apples. They froze on the way home. We ate some of them anyway. That night everyone had terrible stomach cramps and diarrhea. We made a trail to the outhouse. The folks had fun for some time kidding about the midnight parade. It really was some experience for a shy ten year old boy.

It sure was cold. The snow on the level was about three feet deep and the creeks were drifted completely full. The horses packed the snow so that they walked on about a two foot ridge. You couldn't get them off of it because they went almost to their bellies on the flats. They could hardly get out of it in the draws. It was tough but I learned a lot about cows, driving horses, finding my way in a storm and how to think in an emergency--or maybe how to avert one. I certainly didn't miss school.

Today, children get such gifts as a $300 mini self propelled car. That is a very long way from a family with two boys and a girl on a Montana ranch in 1921. For Christmas that year, we boys got a used baseball and an ash club, which had been smoothed real nice and fixed into a very good bat. Each of us got a brand new pair of shoes. Sis got a very pretty, small doll buggy, which had cost $1.09 from Sears and Roebuck. Mom made her a very nice doll to go with the buggy.

Since toys were very scarce, we were free to use our imagination. Being industrious boys, with lots of space, we found things to do that had few instructions. Somewhere we found six .45 caliber pistol bullets. For some reason, known only at that time, we wanted to take the lead out of the shells. Dad had a blacksmith shop with the tools we needed, but it was locked. There had to be a way to get in. We discovered a window, which could be removed, so that we could get to the tools we had to have. I, being the oldest, had to show how it was done.

I found a big chisel, a hammer, and the big anvil. I put the chisel just behind the lead, tapped it a couple of times and the lead came out. Fred had to have his turn. He thought that if a small tap was good, a big tap ought to be better. He put the chisel behind the lead and hit the chisel. There was a great big bang. He dropped the hammer and chisel, grabbed his head and shouted, "I'm shot! I'm shot!"

I was scared. I grabbed his hand and jerked it away to see blood running down his arm. I could see that he had not been hit in the head. A small piece of the metal had gone through the fleshy part of his hand. First things first! We had to take care of the hand. Then (think fast) what should we tell Mom? Luckily, Mom and Sis had not heard the noise, so we reported that Fred had fallen down and cut his hand on a piece of glass. The next thing was to get the shop back to normal. Toys should come with better instructions.

That spring Mom and Dad came home, and we moved onto a vacant ranch. Dad worked for the storekeeper and a few other ranchers. We started to school that year and went about two months. The teacher left. We got another one about the first of March. We went until some time in May. On a nice day in May, we all decided to go to a stock pond and go swimming. Luckily, or unluckily, Dad happened to see us. That was the end of swimming and school for that year.

That fall we moved southwest of Ridge, Montana. The place was owned by the Ridge Postmaster, Mr. Wallace. He had one bad leg. A horse had fallen on it and it had never been set right. He had quite a few cows that Dad fed.

We were at Mr. Wallace's ranch for a year and a half, from 1921 to 1923. My brother was a year and a half younger than I, so we made a pretty good pair. There was a small creek that ran close to the house. There were some small trees and a lot of brush close to the house. There was a blacksmith shop and an old log shed that Dad made into a chicken house. In every chicken house there had to be nests where the chickens could lay their eggs. Oranges came in wooden crates that had a divider in the center. This made two nests. It happened that there was quite a large hole in the divider of one of the orange boxes that Dad had used for nests. The nests were usually anchored about four feet high with a board leading up to them so the hens could walk up to the nests.

For some reason there were a lot of bull snakes around the ranch that year. One had crawled into the hen house. They thrive on eggs of any kind. They have a sense of smell, or some way of knowing where there are eggs. This snake crawled up the board to the nest. It crawled over the end of the box, ate an egg, crawled partly through the knot hole and ate another egg. It sure was in a predicament, because it couldn't go forward or backward. That was where we went to gather eggs. Dad was called in to take the matter in hand. Then there was one less bull snake on the ranch, also two less eggs.

The second bull snake climbed a tree. This was a tree that was leaning at quite an angle. We heard a robin making a great fuss. We knew that something was wrong. We went to explore. The robin was flying through the upper limbs of the tree. It was really doing its best to give the bull snake a rough time. We got the bull snake. That robin sure said thanks for the help.

The third bull snake wanted a cool place. Dad, Fred and I were working in a hay field quite a ways from the house. All at once we saw Mom in the yard waving her apron. We took off on a run to see what was wrong. When we got to the house, we found Mom sitting in the middle of the room with a garden hoe. The kitchen was quite large. In one corner we had a big ice box. It was about a foot off of the floor. There were some jugs and jars under it. The screen door had a crack under it large enough so that the bull snake had crawled under the door. Mom had been outside and had come around the corner just in time to see that snake go under the door. She hadn't had time to see what kind it was. There were some rattle snakes on the prairie, so she took no chances. She got her garden hoe and went into the house. The snake finally poked his head out. She bopped him one, but it wasn't out far enough for her to do much damage. It didn't take long for us boys to make sure it was a bull snake. So another bull snake bit the dust. So much for the snake farm!

We were quite a ways from a store, and we didn't have much money. Anything that helped with the groceries was more than welcome. There was a big barn. It had been taken over by pigeons. There were just three places where they could go in or out. If we could just get a few, Mom could sure make a good pot pie. We waited until quite a few were in the barn. We got a couple of long sticks, plugged up the holes so that the pigeons could not get out. We could climb up quite high. The pigeons would fly by and we would knock one down. We would get three or four, which sure made a good dinner.

Dad added another good dinner. There was a pond at the foot of quite a small hill. One fall day, three ducks landed on the pond. Dad just had a rifle, which was somewhat larger than a twenty two. He knew that if he hit the body of the duck, there wouldn't be much left. He took aim at the green-headed mallard. He neatly clipped the head off. He didn't brag, but I sure thought that that was some shooting.

Dad also trapped coyotes, badger, bobcat, and skunks (whether he wanted to or not). The hides were worth pretty good money. Even skunk hides were worth about $15, which at that time was about a month's wages. One of his trips, Dad caught a skunk in a trap. He shot it and skinned it right where he caught it. He got a long willow to tie to the hide, so he could hold it slightly down wind as he came home.

I was working with two other horses in the barn. Dad started to lead his horse into the barn, when one of the horses smelled the skunk and kicked, knocking Dad down. I was eleven years old and scared stiff. I managed to get out of the way of the horses and reach Dad's hand. I helped him get out. The horse that kicked him had on sharp steel shoes and really crippled Dad up for about three weeks.

During the winter there was plenty of snow for sledding, skiing, snowball fighting and the making of a snowman or two. The biggest problem was getting the equipment. Of course, making a snowman, or having a snowball fight came pretty easy most of the time.

The first sled we had was homemade. It was just two runners with a flat top. The only way you could steer it was by dragging a foot on one side or the other. I don't remember whether the folks finally got us a sled, or whether Grandma and Grandpa got it for us for Christmas. We really used that sled. We found out about dog sleds some way. It certainly wasn't by seeing it on TV or at a picture show. Those things didn't exist for us then.

Fred and I decided that we would see if we could fix up some kind of a harness for our two dogs so that they could pull our sled. Quite often, some one had a cowhide hanging on a fence. The cowhide could be hanging there because the cow ended in any one of several ways. The hides were stiff and hard to cut into strips to make straps out of them.

16

We didn't have the best of knives, but we managed to get enough strips to tie the dogs to the sled.

The older of the two dogs was the one which Dad got for Fred when I started to school. The other was a full grown pup of hers. They were both good with cows. The dogs loved to chase cows. That, of course, was against the rules, unless there was strict supervision, and a reason to move the cows. The folks were gone. The cows were in a pasture quite a ways from the house. We thought that we had everything under control. The snow was pretty deep and crusted, so it was good sledding. We hooked the dogs to the sled and took them out where they could see the cows. We jumped on the sled and yelled, "Go get them!" The dogs knew what we meant. With great glee, the dogs and boys took off. It lasted only minutes for the boys. The sled ran smack into a snow drift, and away went the dogs. Just then the folks came home. They wanted to know why the dogs were chasing the cows. Our explanations didn't seem to fit the occasion too well.

Fred and I repaired our dog harness, but from then on, we had to lead our dog team or get them quite a ways from home and tell them to go home. That didn't have near the excitement that chasing cows did.

When Mom and Dad spent the winter in Hot Springs, they got acquainted with some folks named Brown who had two ranches. One was just out of Custer. The other one was about nine miles out of Hot Springs. They had to have someone run one of them. Dad wrote them a letter to see if by any chance they could use us. Fortunately the job was open.

A bachelor friend of ours, Clem, wanted to leave Montana. Mom couldn't see any reason to stay, so some planning went on. The friend had a team and a saddle horse. Dad had one old mare and a saddle horse. Dad also had a wagon and a double wagon box. He made a deal with my Uncle Bob to use one of his mares until Dad could pay him for it at some uncertain time in the future. Dad fixed a two wheeled wagon trailer with canvas on top. We were ready to leave on Christmas Day. We woke up and great big flakes of snow were coming down. It was about five degrees above zero. There were questions about whether we should start then or not. We did not have much hay or grain for the horses or feed for the twelve old hens we had with us. Nor did we have much food for us. I don't know whether it was out of ignorance or faith, but I said, "We are ready so let's go. This weather can't get any worse."

I guess they thought that if we kids could stand it, then maybe they could, too. So we started out. We had a cold day. The first day Dad rode ahead to see if he could find a place for us to stay. We really got a break. There was a ranch on one side of the road. On the other side, there was a one room school house. It had been used that day for a Christmas program. The heating stove had been banked for the night and was still nice and warm. The stove had a good, big flat top. Mom heated up some stew. Was it ever good!

The next night was just the opposite. We were out on the Wyoming prairie where coyotes howl and rattlesnakes rattle. Dad took off about three o'clock to see if he could find some shelter. It got dark early. He didn't come back for ages. We just kept on going. He finally got back. He had found an old house with a window out. It had an old kitchen range that had some of the top lids missing. We scrounged around and found an old piece of tin that we used for lids. The folks put up a quilt to close a broken window. It was cold that night. There was a haystack in a corral and Dad tied the horses up and fed them. We slept together with our clothes on that night and got an early start the next day.

The next afternoon the mail carrier caught up with us and was he ever hostile! I thought he was going to eat Dad. Dad told him that we had to have a place to stay over night and that he had tried to find a place. He offered to pay him for the hay. The guy cooled off and said that he guessed the horses had not done much damage. Dad didn't need to pay for the hay.

We went on. It was cold! We had a creaky, squeaky wagon. We had an old kerosene lantern that we kept lighted in the canvas covered trailer. It was amazing how warm it seemed to be. Of course, if you come in out of weather that was from 10 below zero to 10 above zero, it doesn't take much to seem warm.

We made 10 or 12 miles a day. Wyoming is a big state anytime. We got to Upton and it turned colder. It went down to 10 below, then 20 below and then 40 below. Luckily, when Mom was ill in Hot Springs, the folks had become acquainted with a doctor who had retired to Upton. He had a large place. His wife had died. He needed something to keep him busy, so he had taken a rural mail route. Dad got in touch with him to see if we could keep the horses at his place until it warmed up a little. That great guy said, "Sure, just move in and take care of the place as long as you want." We stayed a week and a half and the weather warmed up to zero. We went on.

We got just east of Newcastle and stopped to eat a lunch and to feed the horses some oats. A man came along in a Packard car. He was from Custer. He stopped and visited awhile. He found out where we were going. He said he would take Mom and us kids to John Browns. John lived on a ranch about three miles south of Custer. Mom, Sis and my brother went with him. I wasn't about to desert the ship.

That night we stayed at a ranch. They told us that the crossing at Hell's Canyon was real bad. The entrance and exit were real steep and icy. We wanted to get over it in the daylight. Dad was driving the four horse team. The horses didn't have sharp shoes and Dad thought we might have trouble, so we started before daylight. It was farther than we thought and there was no place to stay. We got to Hell's Canyon after dark. There was nothing to do but try. Clem took the lantern. I followed, riding one horse and leading the other two. It was easier to lead the horses that way than to tie them beside or behind the wagon. My hands and feet didn't get frostbite, but I don't know how I kept from it. Dad wanted us just ahead of the lead team. He could tell if there was a slippery spot if the saddle horses were sliding around. If they slipped, it sort of gave Dad a chance to change course a little. We eased our way down that steep grade somehow. That was one long hill that night, but we had no mishap.

There had been an old sawmill at the bottom. There were some sheds where we could put the horses. We had some oats for them but no hay. We let the lantern burn in the trailer that night and slept in all of our clothes.

At daylight the next morning, we started again. In about three hours we got out of the canyon. We went until about nine the next morning. We saw a ranch about a quarter mile from the road. We pulled in there to see if we could get something to eat, and some hay for the horses. Those folks were wonderful. They said, "Put the horses in the barn and corral. We will feed them. Go on in the house. The folks will have something for you to eat in a little while." Dad offered to pay them.

They said, "It is our pleasure. Glad we could help. Just have a good trip the rest of the way."

Those folks were really great! They fed our horses and us. They had home-made sausages, hash browns, eggs, and some biscuits right out of the oven. I'm sure the lady wondered how in the world one small boy could put away so much food. They wouldn't hear of being paid. We made it to what they called Four Mile that evening and on to John Brown's the following day.

We stayed at Brown's about three days and then went to his lower ranch between Pringle and Hot Springs. Dad found a ranch near Pringle. We moved into that place. The school was about three miles from there. We started school that spring and went about six weeks. The teacher left. No more school that year.

The next fall Mom, Sis, and Fred went to Hot Springs. Grandma and Grandpa Crinklaw had moved down there because Grandpa was very feeble. They thought that they might get into the State Home because he had been an Indian Scout. I stayed with Dad on the ranch. I started to the country school.

SCHOOL DAYS

MOST CHILDREN GO TO school to learn. The trouble is that they learn some things other than what is in the books. Some of the country schools had poor attendance because the boys were kept home to help on the farm or ranch. Some of the pupils got to be sixteen or seventeen years old before they graduated from the eighth grade.

This school had some of the boys who were from 14 to 17 years old. It was about the middle of September. It got pretty chilly at night. In the mornings before school, some of the boys would start the fire in the wood stove to warm the school house before the teacher got there. One morning, boys being boys, they got a great idea. They fixed the wood in the stove so that it was ready to light. Then they put some green boughs on the wood. They went up on the school house and plugged the chimney. Then they waited for the teacher to come in sight. When she was within about a quarter of a mile of the school house, they started the fire. By the time the teacher got to the school, there was smoke coming out of every door, window, and crack.

The teacher came up to the boys. She looked them over. Then she said, "Good morning boys. It looks like you are going to have school in a smoke house today!" She turned around and walked away.

For some reason, that was the end of school there for that year.

I had never received a report card. I had been put in the fourth grade in that school. A boy from Hot Springs had visited that school. He was in the fifth grade. After the Christmas break, I went to Hot Springs. When I started school in there, I told them that I was in the fifth grade. I had no report card to substantiate that, but they took me at my word. I was old enough, so there I was.

Before I went to school in Hot Springs, I had never been in a fight. I had been in school there only a week. That Friday night, my brother Fred and I went to a movie. It was dark in the theater. We could just see some kids, but couldn't see who they were. We managed to sit in the row behind four sixth grade boys. The seats in the theater weren't in the best of shape. The one in front of me had a loose board in it. I put my foot on it. It snapped a little. I didn't think anything about it. A little later, in my excitement, I did it again. The boy, who was sitting in that seat, happened to be the toughest boy in the sixth grade. He looked around and saw that it was that fifth grade country kid. He informed me, in no uncertain terms, that I might get away with doing that to a fifth grader, but I wouldn't get away with doing it to a sixth grader. I guess that it sounded like a challenge. Anyway, I reached down and popped the board a couple of more times.

After the show, Fred and I started up the sidewalk to go home. We just got a little ways and here came the sixth grade boys. The one who had been in front of me, said, "I want to see you in the alley."

I said, "I didn't lose anything in the alley," and walked on.

Fred said, "You can't let him get away with that!"

After a few more words, we walked into the alley. I didn't know what to expect. We just got stopped and I got hit. I had thrown up my hands to protect my face. The boy's name was Ralph. He was pretty good at fighting. He was really pouring it on, but he had his head down. I was looking out between my hands. He made a mistake and looked up. It was my chance and I sure took it. I clobbered him in the eye.

Just then two older girls came along. They said, "That's enough." Spoil sports.

I was kind of glad they were there. I think Ralph was glad to have some intervention, also. Ralph had really punched me in the nose and it had bloodied both of us up. We walked up the sidewalk to the hotel. We went in and washed up. Fred and I went home. I had a few bruises around my forehead, but by Monday morning, they were pretty well gone. I still hated to go to school. When I got there and saw Ralph, he had an eye that was swelled plumb shut, and was really black.

I thought, "Well that fifth grade kid hadn't done so bad!"

I had no idea what effect that would have on the school. I guess the word got around school that you don't mess with that country kid. I had no more trouble.

Our teacher's name was Miss Coutes. She was French. She had black eyes and she was tough. The situation here was entirely different than what I was used to. In the little country school, I moved about whenever I felt like it. I went to the outhouse without permission. I talked whenever I pleased. I learned my arithmetic by counting cows. Miss Coutes and I had a little trouble with my language, too. I learned to speak to the cows and horses by listening to older people. She informed me that I was not to use that language in school. Somehow she had enough faith in me to pass me into the sixth grade. I got my first report card saying that I passed a grade in school. Our teacher went into the sixth grade with us. That year I got to be the third from the highest in my grade. There were two girls who ranked higher. I just couldn't beat them. I never worked so hard before or since.

When I was 13, a young fellow named Ray, and I decided that we needed summer jobs. He had a Model T Ford. We had some adult friends, who were running a ranch near Buffalo, Wyoming. Mom had been keeping in contact with them. They said that they could use some help. So Ray, the Model T, and I took off for Buffalo to a job of putting up hay and shocking grain. I helped by mowing and raking hay until that was done. Then I went to a neighbor to shock grain.

In the meantime, I had become acquainted with some ranch neighbor kids. There were five of them; three girls and two boys. I made the sixth kid. They all had access to riding horses. They could furnish me a horse. So after supper the party began.

There was wide open country to explore. We were all good riders and the horses liked to run. We didn't have any idea where we would go. We did a good job of exploring for three nights. I managed to get back by eleven o'clock and to work by seven the next morning. I'm not sure I shocked all the grain that was expected.

On the fourth night, we went to a place where I had never been. I didn't pay enough attention to the way back. Strangely, things don't look the same at night as they do in the daylight. I was lost. We hadn't followed any roads. I finally came to a gate in a fence. I decided that I had better spend the rest of the night there. At least I wouldn't get any farther away from the place where I wanted to be. The ground didn't turn out to be a feather bed. But, somehow even a thirteen year old boy can get tired. It was probably about 4:00 when I woke up.

I found out that I was farther away than I had any idea that I was. I got back to work, without breakfast, at about 8:00. I started in shocking grain. The owner was in another field binding grain. It wasn't very long until he came over to where I was. He said, "You know that you are supposed to start work at seven."

I said, "I had a hard night and was tired."

He didn't mince any words. He just said, "I don't need you any more."

I said, "You don't know what a favor you just did for me." I don't think he liked it very much. At least he didn't call me back.

We lived in a rented house. We did not have inside plumbing. There was a water pump in the yard. The rent was $12 a month. My mother worked in a commercial laundry in Hot Springs. She worked six days a week for $12. We knew a family who lived in Newcastle. They were pretty good friends of ours. The man was a business man who had quite a bit of money. He suggested that Mom might like to have a laundry of her own.

The project didn't go any place very fast. There were several draw backs. Finally Mom decided that I should go to Newcastle and find out as much as I could about the laundry. We didn't have enough money for her to take off work for as long as it would take, so I went instead.

I had a list of about thirty questions and I could think of a lot more. I hitchhiked to Newcastle. Amazingly, luck was with me. A salesman came along and picked me up. I arrived in Newcastle about eight o'clock. For the most part, I got all of the questions answered, some not as I expected. Most people were very friendly and helpful. I could see that running a laundry was going to cost a lot more money than our family was used to handling. That was the way I felt, but of course Mom would make her own choice.

Then, I had to get back home. I had always loved the sound of a train whistle. I had seen men who rode the freight trains. Even though they looked like dirty bums, I still thought that it would be fun to ride on a freight train. It just happened that a freight train was stopped in Newcastle and about ready to head for Edgemont which was on the way to Hot Springs. I thought that was my chance. I hadn't talked to anyone who had ridden a freight train. There was an open car two cars behind the engine. I made the mistake of climbing into that car. No problem! The doors were open on both sides of the car. I didn't think about the fact that there were no stops between Newcastle and Edgemont. When that old coal burner got up steam, the smoke, cinders and ash really poured out. The open doors on the box car made perfect suction for whatever was coming its way. If you have ever been in an open automobile in a sand or sleet storm, you have a pretty good idea of what was going on in that box car.

When I finally got to Edgemont, I went to the river and got rid of some of that top soil. Right then, I knew why the men who road the freight trains looked exactly as they did. I still love the sound of a train whistle. I hitchhiked the rest of the way back to Hot Springs.

Dad sheared sheep in the spring and trapped coyotes in the winter. Later he trapped coyotes and poisoned prairie dogs for the government. The government created an agency which was called The Fish, Game, and Parks Agency. They hired several men in different parts of the country to trap wolves. Later, they added coyotes, prairie dogs, and skunks.

One fall, the skunks invaded the area. Really, what a stink! Of course, no one wanted the job of getting rid of one, let alone a whole bunch of them. Guess who got to be the lucky guy. Dad got his gas mask and went to work. There seemed to be a lot of skunks around the city dump. At that time the dump was not controlled. People brought things at any time. He didn't want anyone to get hurt when he was shooting skunks so he put up a sign that said, "There will be skunk elimination any time after eight pm. Beware! I will not be responsible for accidents."

He knew of a culvert that some of the skunks were using. He knew that he would have to do something to get the skunks out of the culvert. Somebody suggested that he put a hose on the exhaust pipe of his car and plug the other end into the culvert. It sounded like a very good idea.

Dad could stand at the upper end of the culvert with his trusty shot gun and really take care of the skunks as they came out.

That brought up the problem of what time would be the best for getting the most skunks. It turned out to be about five o'clock in the morning. The skunks had a night out and were ready for a rest. They certainly got a surprise and so did Dad. He got all prepared and started the car. Skunks started coughing and coming out as planned. Dad started killing skunks. The skunks kept coming and coming. Dad couldn't believe it. There were twenty-three dead skunks. Even he couldn't believe that the skunks were having a convention. I'm sure that after that disaster, the skunks would decide that the next convention would not be advertised so much.

He got quite a write up in the paper and sure a lot of thanks.

All animals have their natural enemies and develop ways to avoid or deal with them. The deer usually hear, see, or smell trouble and they flee as they are very swift. Horses, donkeys, and mules are very different. Sometimes, horses run. It depends on what the danger is. A stallion would fight a bear if his band of mares was in danger, or if a bear was close to a colt. Sometimes, a stallion would fight to the death if another stallion came close to his band of mares.

A mule is a cross between a donkey and a horse. They could be small or large and have the characteristics of either one. They are the most unpredictable animals that a man ever used. If they, under all kinds of treatment, decide that they would conform, they could be tough work animals.

My brother and I were bringing about twenty horses and one little mule into Hot Springs. The little mule was trailing in the back. There was a big dog standing on a porch a little ways back from the street. I guess he thought that the mule should be afraid of him. He came charging out all puffed up. That little mule laid back his ears, lowered his head and took after that dog. The dog changed course in a hurry. There were about ten steps up to the porch. It didn't look like the dog touched the steps. He just flew up them. I thought that maybe the mule would go up after him. He just turned back and followed the horses.

Several years later, I worked for my step-father on his ranch north of Chadron, Nebraska. Most saddle horses weigh about 1,000 pounds. Bill had a horse that weighed about 900 pounds. His name was Teddy.

The first time that I rode him, he was just three years old. He showed promises of being a good horse. It is hard to tell what any horse of that age may become, because of the treatment which they receive as they grow.

Teddy was a natural cutting horse. From the very first, it was his pleasure to out-maneuver any cow. A lot of horses prefer other activities. Quite a few larger horses like it when you take down a rope and start after a steer or cow. They know that if you tied those critters to the saddle horn that the cow was going to be at the horse's mercy very quickly. Teddy didn't like anything jerking him around. He much preferred to have those animals out in front of him trying to dodge him.

In 1936 there were no big rodeos as there are today. There were quite a few county fairs. The ranchers from the nearby area would bring in a few stock for entertainment. Cattle cutting was one thing the cowboys loved. Horses did a lot of the work at that time. We didn't have trailers, trucks, or three wheelers to do the work. One of the men at the ranch won three saddles riding Teddy.

We kept Teddy up in the winter. We needed a horse to get the milk cows, and to move cows from one pasture, or feed pasture to another. We always put sharp shoes on the winter horses because of the frozen ground. Teddy was the only horse I was ever around that liked having shoes put on. He would almost hold his feet up to help. When I would open the barn door to let him out, he would kick up his heels and run and buck. He was the hardest horse to keep shoes on that I ever shod. He sure knew what those shoes could do for him.

We had to have a special lock on the barn door when Teddy was loose in the barn. Just a hook or a turning lock was too easy for him to figure out.

Teddy was gentle enough for any one to ride, but he was usually much too busy to be used for pleasure riding. He hated to have you try to rope anything. He just the same as said, "That's for somebody else to do."

I never roped in a rodeo, where I would be timed, but I was still pretty good at roping calves and sheep. Calves run pretty straight and do not dodge much. Sheep jumping sage brush are a lot different from calves. That old sorrel horse loved to put me where I could rope a ewe and it made him mad if I missed.

We did things which people of today can't believe. We grew up with horses. If horses ran free on the range for three years without being handled, they became wild. Then the horses were brought into a corral and separated into small bunches in other corrals. Then they were roped one at a time. A halter was placed on their heads and they were tied to a post. They were left there to fight being tied until they found that it did no good. Then the handler took a saddle blanket or gunny sack and started getting the horse used to things moving around them. Those horses had nasty teeth and hoofs and they were not averse to using them. Dad broke a lot of horses. He knew how to get along with them.

I worked on a ranch in the summer after we moved to Hot Springs. I worked in June, July and August and made $45 with room and board. I bought all of my winter clothes including shoes. During the school year, I discovered football.

I played football from the time I was a freshman. I only spent part of the time out of any of the games in all four years. I played both offense and defense. I weighed 125 pounds when I was a freshman. Since I had wrestled horses and calves, I was quite tough. I had no problem getting on the team. We had to play all of the time we could. Since there were so few of us, we had to play both on offense and defense. We didn't have a doctor at any of the meetings officially. I missed only about thirty minutes of playing in all four years of football. When I was a junior, I weighed 145 pounds. We played Rapid City that year. I played end against a tackle who weighed 190 pounds. In the third quarter I was hit and lost consciousness. The first thing that I knew, I was on the sideline and the coach was rubbing my neck. I don't know how long I was unconscious but I heard the coach ask me if I was all right. We were ahead of Rapid City and I guess he wanted it to stay that way. I didn't think that I was that important, but I got back in the ball game for the fourth quarter. We won 21 to 6.

A lot of our team graduated that year. The next year, still weighing 145, I played fullback for both offense and defense. That year we played the Pine Ridge Indians. The coach told us, "You guys had better get the jump on them. If they get the first touch down, you probably won't see them for the rest of the game."

I had a little experience with the Indians. I knew they didn't like rough physical contact. I was playing full back and the quarterback gave me the ball. I didn't run around anybody. I tried to run through them. I just hit them as hard as I could. I tried to break in two anyone with whom I came in contact. I was as hard as nails from working in the hay field all summer. The Pine Ridge boys did not like that much. I played too rough. They didn't like that, so instead of trying to stop me they would grab at me, but they stayed out of my way. We got to about 30 to nothing. The coach pulled me out and said, "What are you trying to do, run them off the field?"

I said, "Before the game, you said that we had better get the jump on them. That was exactly what I was doing."

Our next target was Sturgis. One of our best challengers. They were just about our size. To add to the competition, their coach was our coach's brother-in-law. I had gained a little weight, so that I was up to about 150 pounds. The coach put me in as fullback. I was pretty fast, but still very light for fullback. They thought that it was their turn to put us in our place. We were just as determined to show them that we still had a football team. We got on the field and played in the middle of the field until late in the fourth quarter. We got the ball on about the thirty yard line. Since I was the fullback, I was carrying the ball. I found out that I could make yardage by alternating sides just off center. I got my team to hold one side, if I was going the other way. It worked until we got to their twenty yard line. I told the guys, "They are going to plug the line for me. If the quarterback would go real low and hide the ball, then turn as if he was going to give it to me, then went outside of the tackle, I don't think that anyone would stop him." It worked and he made the touchdown. We missed the extra point.

Sturgis got the ball back and was trying to do the same thing to us, but they ran out of time. We beat them six to nothing. It was a very happy bunch of players going home that day.

I also liked to play basketball. I was small compared to most high school boys, so I was not particularly good at it. My hands were not very large, so it was hard to control a basketball. Most of the basketball team was taller than I was. I got to go on every trip, but I did not get to play often. When I was a junior, some of the taller boys graduated. So, when I was a senior, I got to play more often. We didn't have a big team, but they were pretty fast.

Fred (right) and I with our 1931 high school football team

Sturgis was our big challenge. They were just about our size and comparable in skill. We had beaten them in football, so they really wanted to take us in basketball. We were playing at Sturgis. The ceiling to their gym was quite low. I played guard, so I usually shot from quite far out. When we were warming up, I shot fairly long shots. I found out that when I shot from one certain place on the floor, I could quite often make a basket. The shots didn't look like they would go in because they almost hit the ceiling but I put a spin on them and in they went.

We were playing hard and the lead had changed several times. I was on the bench. The coach finally put me in. Sturgis missed a shot. I saw it and started for the basket. I was out almost to the center line in the clear. I got the ball and took about two dribbles in my spot. I relaxed, put the ball where it should be and in it went.

By all the laws of physics, it should have gone under the basket. However, that wasn't where I usually got to shoot. It was just two points because we didn't have the three point rule. I could have gone and sat down because it sure set the regulars on fire. We beat Sturgis by four points. I just made the one basket. I heard the Sturgis coach tell our coach, "If you have luck, you don't have to have good players." I wasn't that good, however that was one basket that really counted for me! I was the only player to make one hundred percent of my shots!

I needed two credits to graduate with my class in 1932. I quit algebra in my freshman year and didn't make up the credits I needed to graduate when I was a senior. I talked to the coach about what I should do. He said that if I was interested, I could come back the next fall, get my two credits, and go on the football and basketball trips. As jobs were scarce and I didn't have any money, I decided that was a good deal.

I went back that fall but was ineligible to play sports. The darned kids elected me as the main cheer leader. I told them that I would not be a cheer leader under any circumstances. I was a good ball player and I got along well with all of the kids. That made me popular, and they wanted me for their leader. Teen-agers can be most persuasive. I put them off. I thought—maybe after awhile. I was hoping that a miracle would happen. I was terrified to get up in front of people!

Just before the first football game, I finally decided that I would do something. We had a study assembly where all of the kids come to a big room for a thirty minute study period. I went to talk to the coach. He heard my story and agreed that I could do as I planned. I borrowed his starting pistol and one blank shell. I got one of the boys to take the pistol. I told him that when I got ready to go up on the stage, he should come to the back of the stage and fire that pistol.

There were three steps going up to the stage. I didn't know whether I could get up them or not. My knees felt like rubber and I was shaking so badly that I could hardly hold onto the papers that contained the yells I wanted them to practice. Needless to say, when that gun went off, it got everyone's attention.

I said, "You wanted a cheer leader, now you have one. You know some of the yells from last year. Now I want you to raise this roof!" They sure did! I just kept putting the pressure on them. I told them that they better have a pretty good excuse if they didn't come to every meeting. That meant every kid in high school.

We got some new yells and we organized a snake dance through the streets down town before every game. The kids really worked and the whole town got behind us. It was a good season. Best of all for me, I found out that I could climb those three steps.

Dad had sheared sheep for years before I started to shear with him. I started on the 25th of May in 1929. I was seventeen years old. Dad had cut the back part off a model T Ford touring car and built a small box on it. He had a gasoline motor to power his clippers. The clippers were like an enlarged pair of hair clippers. There were swinging arms that extended out from the motor so that several men could use the same motor.

Dad and I usually sheared the smaller bunches of sheep, up to about 500 head. If there were more than that, we had four or six men in the crew.

If you have never been around sheep, especially in hot weather in an enclosed shed or barn, you have missed a very penetrating experience. Hot weather is definitely the best time to shear sheep. They have an oil in the wool which gets thin when it is hot and the clippers slide through the wool easily.

It is hard to describe some of the places people expect you to shear sheep. The arrangement of the barn or shed and the pens made a big difference in how many sheep you could shear in a day.

It was customary for the owners of the sheep to feed the shearers. Needless to say, there were as many variations of food as there were differences in flocks of sheep. There are many stories that I remember from the four years I sheared sheep with Dad.

One of them was when four of us were shearing about 1,500 head of sheep southwest of Custer. It was prohibition time so it was illegal to sell or buy whiskey. That didn't stop boot-legging. There was a still near New Castle. The owner of the sheep and his herder went there and got a gallon of whiskey. The sheep herder was staying in an old house about a mile from the owner's house. The owner didn't have room for us in his house, but said that we could stay with the herder.

The herder got drunk. He got a pistol out of his coat in the closet. He was fumbling around with it, which sure wasn't a good idea. Finally he put it back and went outside. Dad got the pistol. The guy came back in. The first thing he did was to look for the gun. Dad said, "You aren't going to get it back tonight."

The herder went back outside again. Dad and one of the fellows got up and stood by the door. The herder stepped back in with a double-bitted axe. Our guy grabbed the axe and Dad grabbed the herder around the arms and threw him on the bed. They held him there for a little while and he passed out. The next morning he had no idea what had happened. We had no more trouble shearing the sheep. We sheared at that place only the one year.

We got another shearing job in the hills south of Custer. It was a different story. The folks had about 300 head of sheep. We had never sheared their sheep before. When they asked if we could do it, Dad managed to work them in between some of the larger bunches, so it was just he and I to shear them. We got to their place about 6:00 in the evening. They were looking for us and had a real nice meal ready.

They had one boy who was about 12 years old and one about 10. I don't know where the father was, but the boys were to corral the sheep. The sheep must have been quite far away, because it was after dark when we heard them coming. The boys had to bring the sheep fairly close to the ranch and put them in a small pasture. There were hills and timber. If sheep don't want to go someplace they take quite a lot of persuasion.

The boys were both on horses. The youngest boy was quite a ways away, but we could hear him chasing the sheep. The older boy was sitting on his horse and doing nothing except calling to his brother, "Danny! Hoot at 'em!" The night was still except for the sheep. The older boy had a deep voice which carried well and echoed in the night. I can still hear, "Danny! Hoot at 'em!"

I don't know how they managed to get the sheep in the pasture, but they were ready to be sheared the next morning.

We were sleeping in the hayloft of the barn. When things quieted down, the frogs from a nearby pond set up their chorus. Something was really different about the sound than I had ever heard. There seemed to be one frog that had a louder, deeper voice. It was just outstanding. I decided that I had to see if I could find that frog. Frogs are very sensitive to any kind of movement. I knew that it was unlikely that I could get near to that one. I started around the pond, quite a ways from the shore. I got about half way around the pond when all of their noise stopped. I continued to search the pond banks. I found a can imbedded in the bank with the open end toward the pond. The can was about the size of a one pound coffee can. The next night, I knew where I was going and what to look for. I was very careful and got to where I could just see the can. The big frog was in the can putting forth his evening concert. I thought this is where amplifiers originated. That was one place we enjoyed shearing sheep.

There were all kinds of people who owned sheep, and all kinds of places where they lived. In one place, a fellow had just bought 1,000 head about two months before shearing time. He was short tempered and thought that everything should move when he said jump. He knew nothing about shearing sheep. He built a high, woven wire corral behind what had been a big barn. He made a few pens in the barn, but no chutes leading up to it. There was just a small door. No sheep could be expected to go into a dark hole. When it was time to start shearing, Shorty, and a couple of other fellows tried to put the sheep in the barn. They would not go in. We had a medium sized, part Husky, dog. Shorty shouted, "Will that dog chase sheep?"

We said, "Yes, but we have to keep him on a leash, because he is too rough." He said, "Turn him loose!" We did. When he got in the middle of the sheep, they were ready to climb the wall of that barn. Anyone who cared for their sheep would never have turned that dog loose with them. Needless to say, Shorty did not have sheep that next spring.

Sheep shearing was a unique job. There were many wonderful people who made the job worth while. On the other hand, it was at best a dirty, hot, smelly, uncertain job that interfered with any kind of steady work. I sheared with Dad for four years. I decided that I had had enough. When we finished that spring, I gave Dad my shearing equipment and said, This is it! I won't be with you next spring."

He said, "Keep it. You will be back." I said, "No way! If there isn't a better way to make a living, then I'll starve."

Later, I did go back to help Dad for one season, and I also sheared five hundred of my own sheep. On the second year that I had my own sheep, I had two other fellows shear them. One of them had sheared sheep with Dad and me some thirty-five years before.

ON MY OWN

IFOUND THERE WERE A lot of jobs much preferable to shearing a bunch of stinking sheep. I worked on a dairy that summer and winter until school started because I still needed money. I talked with Bob, a World War Veteran who delivered our milk. He, his wife, and their 12 year old son ran a small dairy. They really needed help. Bob had been gassed in the war. At times, he could hardly breathe. They felt guilty to offer me a job for just my room and board. It was a job every day of the week. However, I was glad to be making my own way. I worked for them for a year and a half.

I had a buddy who had joined the National Guard which was called the Home Guard back then. They paid $4 for a meeting once a week. That was big money. What a temptation that was. My friend thought that I was stupid to not go with him. He finally did talk me into joining. I took all of the shots. I don't know why they gave me all of the shots before they had my name on the paper to say that I had joined. Later, I decided that that was just the way the government did things. Anyway, I was all ready to sign up. I went down to the meeting. It was in the auditorium. There was a dumb kid, who couldn't count to ten, marching the troops up and down the floor. He was in the wrong place. He should have been training animals for the circus. Anyway, I sure didn't think that I needed that sort of training. I got out of there in a hurry.

My buddy got to me the next morning. He said, "How come you didn't come down last night and sign up?"

I said, "I didn't sign up last night and that is just the half of it. I'm not going to sign up any time."

That was just the first time I escaped a crisis. The second time was about a year later. Another buddy and I decided that we would like to be airplane pilots. Lincoln, Nebraska had an air base where they were giving flying lessons. It took us quite a while to get ready to leave. Some way my buddy got convinced that he should not go to the school. I think that his mother was afraid that that he might learn more things than just flying an airplane, and she wouldn't be there to tell him how to do it. I debated for quite while about what I should do. Finally the lack of money made my decision for me.

I ended up working for a rancher until November 11th, 1933. I went to Hot Springs. One evening, a neighbor boy asked me if I would like to go to a show with him. We went to the show. As we were walking home, the Police Chief stopped to ask us if we wanted a ride home. He was a good friend of mine. He asked us what we were doing. I said that I had just come home from working on a ranch. They did not need me any more for the rest of the winter. He asked us if we wanted to go into the Civilian Conservation Corp. The other boy said that he wasn't interested. I said, "Just give me a chance."

He said, "There are some boys going Monday morning. The quota is full, but if anyone drops out, I am sure that you would have a chance of going. If you want to try, just be at the court house at 7:00 on Monday morning. Monday morning I was in the CCC.

Joining 200 young guys in a camp was a new experience for me. The Army was in charge of the camp, and the Forest Service was in charge of the work. On the first morning, all newcomers were issued axes. I practically grew up with an axe. The axes came in boxes of eight. There were just two left when it came to me. One had a dark mark where the handle went into the axe head and another on the end of the handle. The man in charge said that he would give me a different one, but that was just the one I wanted. It was already marked.

It took me very little time to sort out the people in charge. I had been around long enough to find out where the bums came from. One boy from Sioux Falls, who hadn't been around a great deal, went to work in the laundry. Some wise guy told him that they needed an underwear stretcher, which had been borrowed by someone. The guys in the laundry thought that it was a great joke to send him all over camp looking for an underwear stretcher. He went out. After about an hour and a half, he showed up back at the laundry. He told the guys that he had gone to all of the places he had been told to look. He said that at the last place where he went, they told him that some one had wanted to stretch a board and ruined the stretcher. He said that they would just have to order a new one, because he knew that they would sure have to stretch their underwear.

That was just the start. Some of the other fellows decided that it was time to fix the guys at the laundry. They scrounged around and found some very large, old, dirty underwear. They wrapped it up nicely, and put a note in it saying. "As you are good at cleaning things up, we are sure that you can handle this. If you can find a few more like it, you will not need a stretcher." They also spread the word to not associate with the guys from the laundry, because they were too big for their underwear.

These things which didn't happen, led to my decision to go to Chadron State Teachers College to see if I could become a teacher and a coach. Money would again play a part in what would happen. My mother had married Bill Ormesher and was living in Chadron. I could stay with her. I saved $60 that summer.

I enrolled in the college. Since I had missed so much school in the lower grades, I was having a real rough time in English class. My teacher asked me if I would like a little help. I was having so much trouble that I certainly would like to have someone rescue me. There a cute young girl majoring in English who was working for the teacher, so she was assigned the task. Her name was Alberta. My $60 only lasted the first two semesters. I had to find a job.

I went to work for Bill at the ranch on the seventh day of March, 1935. There had been a bad storm about a week before. The snow was about two feet deep on the level. Bill had about 1,100 head of steers north of the ranch. It had warmed up and then froze, making a crust on top of the snow. The steers couldn't get any grass.

On the eighth day of March, another fellow and I started hauling hay and scattering it close to the stacks so the steers could get to it. We used pitch forks as we didn't have tractors with hay forks at that time.

We started at daybreak and continued until it was dark. It looked like there was enough hay to last a week. They brought the steers in there about nine that night. The next morning it didn't look like we put any hay out.

We had a cake cart and hauled about fifteen sacks of cotton seed cake out every day. We also fed them six loads of hay every day. On Sunday, the 15th of March, we started to round up the steers to feed them their cake.

Bill had some big dams on the creek. It had been warm for a couple of days. The ice had honey-combed and was rotten. It was about three feet thick. About 25 head of steers crowded out on one of the dams and broke through. Bill happened to be very close. I was riding a big brown horse that was very good on a rope. I was quite a ways away, but I saw Bill jumping up and down waving his hat. I knew there was some trouble. I raced down there. By that time, Bill had a steer roped. I wrapped the end of the rope around the saddle horn and pulled the steer out. The second one I pulled out broke the cinch on the saddle. One of the other boys jerked the saddle off his horse and gave it to me. We got all of the steers out. I think the last ones were bothered by a slight case of hypothermia.

Bill had a lot of big dirt dams on his land and they had to be repaired every fall. That is when I learned to drive a caterpillar tractor. The water would wash away some of the dirt. It would leave a cut bank on the upper side. This was from about a foot to three feet high and would eventually wash out. I started repairing the dams with four horses and a "fresno". This was a kind of a road scraper. It wasn't long until that seemed too slow. We updated to a caterpillar tractor and a "tumblebug" which was another kind of scraper. There were seven men working for Bill and none of us had ever been on a tractor like that before.

Bill went to Chadron to get a man who knew how to run it. He found a young man, who was an "expert" and who "knew all about tractors". Bill took the tractor and the young man up to a short dam to start out. On the lower end of the dam was a pretty good sized mud hole. I have no idea why the young man got close to it, but he got the tractor stuck in the mud. He was only there half of the day but that was long enough for him to stick the tractor and get a track off. We discovered he didn't know much about tractors or Nebraska gumbo. Bill took him back to town. On Sunday morning, he got a state man, who was experienced with tractors, to come out and help us get the tractor back in working condition. When we finished, Bill said to me, "Henry will be here in the morning to help and you can start repairing dams."

I said, "Man, I have never been on one of these things!" He said, "You can't start any younger." Sometimes, I wondered if I was going to learn any older.

That first short dam went ok. The second dam was a long one. It had a lot of water behind it and was washed pretty bad. I worked on it about a day and had quite a bit of loose dirt on the upper side. I got a little too far over, when the tumblebug hooked into some solid dirt and the tractor headed for the water. I shut it off and went over the upper side. I didn't even take time to say, "If you want a swim, go ahead." It didn't get to the water. To this day I don't know how I kept that thing from turning over or how I kept from burying it in the dam. Some of the dams were plenty deep enough.

We got another tractor and put it on the lower side of the dam. We hooked a cable from it to the front of the caterpillar. Then Bill said, "Get on it and drive it out."

I did. I worked a lot of hours on that old cat. However, after working twelve or fourteen hours on it, you didn't always quit driving it when you went to sleep. It wasn't long until one night, I came straight up in bed grabbing for levers. I am not sure that this would qualify as a nightmare. I always thought that a nightmare would be connected to a horse. In any case, there were many nights that I woke up in a cold sweat grabbing for levers. Alberta even rode on the tractor behind me for several miles. She learned as much about ranching as I did about English.

Alberta graduated with a degree in high school English and Speech. There were no jobs open for that anywhere. She took a job in a rural school near Hot Springs. My mother met Alberta and felt that she was much nicer than the other girls I dated once in a while. She managed to get us together a few times in the next two years. I kept on working on the ranch.

It seemed that every weekend there were cattle to move, brand, vaccinate, or separate to sell. Relatives and "would be cowboys" came out from town to help. It fell to the regulars to finish up the dirty work, which came in abundance.

When I first went to work for Bill, I made the fifth man working for him. There were two brothers from Texas. The older one, Bob, was about 25 years old. He weighed about 135 pounds. He had been married quite young. He was pretty well educated. He had been the manager of a lumber yard. He was making pretty good wages for that time. He had a small daughter of whom he was very proud. However, he said that his former wife could spend money much faster than he could make it. She had gotten him into financial troubles over his head. He said, "They didn't run me out of Texas, they just followed me to the border trying to get me to come back."

His brother, Woody, was about 20 years old. He wanted to be a cowboy, so he followed his brother. He was about six feet tall, broad shouldered and he could move like a cat.   However, unless pushed, he looked like he was in slow motion. He was very friendly and nice to be around. Then there was Harley. He was an older gentleman, who lived in Chadron. He was a quiet, good worker and was pretty easy to get along with. Jack was the odd ball. He was probably about 25 years old. He was quite large. He must have weighed about 200 pounds. He didn't like horses. He was a good mechanic and was in his glory all greased up. Not being a horse person, sort of put him by himself. He was a good worker, and it was usually not too hard to get along with him. Once in a while, he would get a moody streak and would get ornery. Then he had to be calmed down.

About that time I came on. I was the step-son of the boss and right out of college. Where did I fit in? I had been around quite a bit among some pretty rough customers. I only weighed about 150 pounds. I kept a low profile, but didn't back up much. I very soon found out that being the step-son of the boss had a few advantages, but more disadvantages. The first thing was to put Jack straight. It wasn't a week until he accused me of running to Bill with something. I looked him straight in the eye and said, "If there is anything going on between you and me, that's the way it is. Bill has nothing to do with it. You had better not go jumping to conclusions." That was an important step, as it turned out. I had no trouble getting along with the men. However, if someone found a job he didn't like, it seemed as though he could get real busy doing something else. Bill had said to me that I should take care of whatever needed doing. He had more confidence in me than I had.

The first summer that I was at the ranch, Woody, Jack, Harley and I were putting up hay at another ranch of Bill's. We each had a team and a hay rack. We would leave the team there and go back to the main ranch. In the morning, we would feed the horses, harness them and get ready to go to work. There was a windmill near where we were working. The brake had broken on the windmill, so that it could turn all of the time. Jack decided to turn it off. He didn't know what had to be done. He climbed up the windmill and decided that he needed a piece of wire to fix it. In his demanding way, he yelled, "One of you guys get me a piece of wire." Nobody jumped at his command. He started fussing at Harley. I finally went and got him a piece of wire. That didn't stop Jack. He kept giving Harley a bad time.

Woody spoke up. He said, "Well Jack, if you want to pick on somebody, pick on me and business will be picking up."

When we got our loads of hay, we pulled in to the hay stack, one on each side, to unload. I figured that if Jack and Woody pulled in at the same time, there could be fireworks. I managed it so that Woody and Harley would pull in at the same time. That left Jack and me to come in together. Just after Jack and I pulled in, Jack stuck his pitch fork into the hay and said, "What would you do? Would you quit and lick the whole damned outfit?"

I laughed at him. I said, "Jack, you couldn't lick one half of that Texan. If you tied into him, you would think that you had a wildcat by the tail and you couldn't turn him loose fast enough, let alone handle the rest of the outfit. It was a good idea to fix the windmill, but you sure didn't have any reason to blow up over a little piece of wire."

I started pitching hay and so did Jack. By night, nothing unusual had happened. We finished that job. Woody went back to riding. Jack went back to his grease. I went back to mowing hay at the ranch.

It was about a week later, when we had to bring in 300 cows and calves from the big pasture to vaccinate for anthrax. Anthrax was a big threat for cattle back then. But the ranchers just took it as another nuisance. The vaccine really took effect, but it had to be used at the first sign of trouble and the dead carcasses had to be burned.

The day we vaccinated the cows was a very long day. We started before daylight and finished after dark. The next day wasn't much better, because moving the cows made some of them lose their calves. It was a big job getting them back together again. Woody's brother was riding all of the time. After the vaccinating of the cows, Woody went back to riding again.

Bill hired two more men to work in the haying.

One day, when I was raking hay, I had a pretty touchy team of horses to drive. One of them was in the habit of reaching down to grab a bite of hay, then he would jump. This time, when he did it, the neck yoke broke, letting the tongue of the rake hit the ground. It threw me under the rake. I really held onto the lines. I twisted and got between two teeth of the rake. Then I let the team go. They just went a little way before they broke loose from the rake. That was the only time that I ever had a run away team, and it would have to be on a darned hay rake.

Bob and Woody stayed at a cow camp which was on leased Reservation land. It was not far from Pine Ridge. It was a pretty lonely job. It was not a real hard job, but to me, it was boring. I guess that it was to Woody also. There were some places nearby where they held dances. He had a girl in Texas who wrote to him about every other week. He would write a letter once in awhile. There was a girl or two from the reservation who got interested in Woody. He decided that he had better do something about it. He came to the ranch. I just happened to be with Bill when Woody came in. They visited a little then Woody said to Bill, "Well Bill, I'm goin' back to Texas. If someone comes lookin' fer me, I sure would like it if you didn't know the direction I went." That seemed to be the break up of the guys.

Bill owned or leased about 15,000 acres of land. We didn't haul our horses around in fancy trailers. We rode them to the far reaches of the ranch and back again at night. One time we left fairly early. It was about five in the morning. Bill said that we wouldn't be gone too long so we wouldn't need any extra horses. I was riding a young horse and knew that I had better take another horse or I might walk back. I took another good, older horse. By eleven my young horse was played out. I switched to the older horse and cut cattle until about six that night. Bill had a big horse that was really tough. He rode him all day. When he got back to the pasture gate, which was about a mile from home, he unsaddled his horse and walked in.

We took 1,186 steers to the railroad in Chadron one time. They shipped them to Tacoma, Nebraska on the railroad. It was before trucks started hauling large loads of cattle.

Bill put up hay the summer he was 75. I came back to see the folks. I was there when Bill said, "This is it. Someone else can put up the hay next year."

It was an interesting and very educational four years. Over the years, I rode a lot of wonderful horses. I also rode some that should have been coyote feed when they were born. There was just no way you could get them to cooperate. The best thing to do was to sell them. I was hard to convince. I treated them too well, and it was a wonder that I didn't get killed by one of them.

One difficult one was a small, pretty sorrel. He would buck but he wasn't too hard to ride. The fellow who had owned him had cinched him real tight and made him sore. I thought that I could get along with him if I handled him very carefully. I moved my saddle back and didn't tighten the cinch very much. I rode him for about half a day and got along fine. Then, all at once, he decided to dump me. The saddle and I went over his head. We went close to a barbed wire fence. The fellow we were with thought that we were going into the fence. He rode between me and the fence just as I hit the ground. His horse jumped me and knocked my horse out of the way. I hit my face on my knee and messed up my face. I got up and tightened the cinch on my saddle. By the time I got back to the ranch, I was fed up with that horse. I knew why that other guy's saddle was so tight!

While Alberta and I were both in Chadron, we got together once in a while. When I went to the ranch, it was different because I had no way to go anywhere. After about two months, I had saved about $40, enough to make a down payment on a car. I bought a 1926 Chevrolet coup.

Alberta's brother Arthur, was going with a girl named Edith who lived in Hemingford, Nebraska. Arthur was working in the radio business and was about as hard up as I was. For awhile, we would drive to Hemingford, pick up Edith and drive the 120 miles to Rapid City, to see Alberta. As soon as we got off work on Saturday, we would get Edith. Then we went to Rapid. We returned home on Sunday evening and went back to work on Monday morning. One Saturday evening,

Arthur and I with my wrecked car

we went to Hemingford to pick up Arthur's girl friend. The roads were graveled. The gravel wasn't put on very well so the county was in the process of putting on some more. The gravel was in a row on one side of the road. It cut the road to about a lane and a half. A big Oldsmobile coup came over the hump in the road. Art was driving my car. There wasn't time for the two cars to slow down, so they locked front wheels. The impact propelled my car upside down onto the gravel row. The car slid down the row for about 25 feet and gently tipped over. It shook us up but didn't seriously hurt any of us. The other car just spun around and went on down the road. It totaled my coup. I had no insurance. I don't know what it did to the other car. We didn't have to report an accident at that time. The other folks took care of their car and that was it. I didn't have another car for quite awhile.

BRINGING HOME THE BACON

ALBERTA AND I WERE married on October 15, 1938 at the Episcopalian Church in Rapid City. Arthur and Edith were married with us in a double ceremony. We stayed at the ranch house for awhile. Bill got one half of a refrigerator railroad car. We made it into a nice one room cabin. It was too well insulated. We were living in it the next winter. We had a little coal oil heater which wasn't vented. We made the mistake of closing the windows tight. We went to bed one night. I woke up because I couldn't get enough air. I was used to being out of doors and getting lots of fresh air. It was a good thing. I don't think that Alberta would ever have known what happened. The stove had burned all of the oxygen out of the air. We sure remedied that in a hurry.

Our little house was across the yard from the ranch house. There had been an old hen house off to the side. We had torn it down. The lumber was still piled there. One night I was going to the ranch house. I saw a skunk go under the old lumber pile. I called to Bill to bring out a flashlight and his shotgun. He did. I held the flashlight and he shot the skunk. We went over to the ranch house for another hour or so. Then we went back to our house and went to bed. In about fifteen minutes we heard squealing and a commotion under the house. There was a terrible odor. We instantly knew that we had a skunk under the house. We had to pick up our young son and head for the ranch house again. The next morning I went out and there was a dead skunk under the lumber pile.

Alberta, Glen, and I in our trailer

There was also a dead skunk under our house. One skunk must have been directly behind the other, so we didn't see it. The shot killed the first one and plastered the head of the second one. It had life enough left to go under our house before it died. I did everything I could think of to get the smell out of the house. It took a month before we could stand it

Our oldest son Glen was born in Rapid City, South Dakota on August 26, 1939. Alberta had been in Rapid City with her mother for about a week. Glen was born about four in the morning. Alberta's brother, Fred, lived in Chadron at the time. He came out to the ranch and told me that Alberta had gone to the hospital. I later learned that he had expected me to jump and hurry to Rapid City. I took my time and stopped at my sister's in Hot Springs for breakfast. I couldn't do much when I got there so what was all the hurry. Alberta was just getting back to normal when I got there, and Glen didn't seem to mind a bit.

We left Bill's the next spring to go to Uncle Bob's in Montana. He had a few cows and about 3,500 head of sheep. Alberta's brother, Everett, and I went up there the first of April. It had snowed and rained and the gumbo was soft. We got about two miles from Uncle Bob's and got stuck. We got a tractor to pull us out and stuck the tractor. We had to wait three days until it froze enough to get them out. We left there about 4:00 in the morning.

I went back to Chadron and loaded up all our stuff on a Chevrolet half ton pickup. We started back to Montana on the seventh of April. We got to Alzada, Montana and it was raining. It sure didn't look promising. I had knobby tires on the pickup. I put on chains because, at Alzada, we went onto a country road which wasn't graveled. We made it to Uncle Bob's turn off.

There was a gate that had been open when I was up there before. Now it was closed. I knew that if I stopped I would be stuck. I was afraid that if I ran through the gate, I would knock out my headlights. I stopped and I was stuck. It was about two miles to Uncle Bob's place. It was as black as a night can get. I sure hated to leave that pickup with Alberta and Glen in it. There were some deep ruts leading to a ranch and I knew that as long as I stayed in those ruts I wouldn't get lost. I made it and got a fellow with his tractor and lantern. The tractor didn't have any lights on it. We pulled the truck out. I just went about ten blocks and got stuck again. The tractor was behind, so he hooked onto me again. It was about 1:00 in the morning when we finally got to the ranch.

We got up about 6:00 the next morning and went on down to Uncle Bob's. I took Alberta down there, left her and all of our belongings and went out to the sheep camp.

There were two fellows out there lambing out 3,500 sheep. I had never lambed sheep before, although I had sheared them for about six years. Luckily, I knew something about horses and most animals. I had a cousin and another young man who soon got me in the groove.

That many sheep had to run on the open range. We did have corrals and a shed that would hold about 50 ewes, but not quite 3,000. The worst part about the whole thing was that it rained. It rained for about 16 days and nights. It even snowed part of the time. You may know something about rain and gumbo, but you know nothing about it unless you have been in Wyoming or Montana in the spring.

We each had two horses. We had some small sheep tents. They were about three feet square and about three feet tall. If a ewe had a problem with claiming her lamb, we would catch her and put her and the lamb in the tent for awhile. We got so that we were pretty good sprinters when catching the sheep and lambs, but about half of the time we had to have some help from our horses and a good rope. The worst time was in the morning from daylight until about 10:00. Just try to sort out about 75 crazy old ewes and 95 lambs. We did it! It was nice if we could get a ewe to claim two lambs.

We had to divide the sheep into four different bunches. The big bunch was made up of the sheep which did not yet have their lambs. The second bunch contained the ewes which we expected would have their lambs that night. The third bunch was made up of ewes that each had one lamb. The sheep in the fourth bunch each had two lambs. Another cousin would come with a pick-up and take them to the ranch.

I put in a lot of time testing my ability to out-think horses. My uncle had two young horses that he had started to break. They had become gentle enough so that they were broke to lead, and you could harness them without getting kicked out of the barn, if you were careful. After a young horse was broke to lead, they were tied to a good gentle horse to learn how to work. Two of his young horses had reached the place where we were working them together.

I had tied them in the barn over night. I got them ready to go to work. I had long halter ropes on them. I had to lead them to the creek to get a drink. The bank to the creek was long, sloping and muddy. I was close beside one of the horses, with the halter rope of the other horse in my hand. On the slick slope, they started sliding, which pulled on the halter ropes. This started me to slip, also. It scared the horse next to me. I knew that he was going to kick. I couldn't get away far enough, so I jumped right up against him. That way, he lifted me with the upper part of his leg. He boosted me about fifteen feet into the middle of the creek. I landed on my feet, which was lucky, because I had the wind knocked out of me and the water was about waist deep.

Alberta saw the commotion from the house. She grabbed Glen and came running down the hill just in time to see me land in the creek. She hollered, "Are you hurt? Are you hurt?" I didn't have breath enough to answer. I could understand her concern.

I worked those two horses the rest of the summer and they turned out to be a real good team.

At Uncle Bob's, I had two wonderful helpers. One was a horse, the other one was a dog. Plodding around in the mud and running down those wild ewes wore out our horses. I told Uncle Bob that we needed another horse or two. He said, "I have a big horse over with some other horses. You may have him if you wish, but you can't keep him from coming home." Most horses of that time were trained to stand if the bridle reins were down. However, some of them learned to drag the bridle reins to the side and you couldn't catch them. This old sorrel horse was smart. If he got a chance, he left you on foot. His name was Croppy.

I told Uncle Bob to bring him over. We had some cube cakes that are like big, really hard fig newtons, which we fed to horses and cattle. I filled my pockets with those cubes. I didn't give that horse a chance to leave me for awhile. Every time I got around him, I would give him a couple of cubes and a pat. In a week, I had that old horse following me around.

Uncle Bob came over to see how we were getting along. The first thing he said was, "I haven't seen old Croppy at the ranch."

I said, "I don't think that you are going to see him over there. Come on over to the corral."

We went to the corral and called to Croppy. He pricked up his ears and trotted over. He knew there was a good chance of getting a pat or two and probably at least a couple of cubes. I gave him a cube. I opened the gate and he followed me to where the saddle and bridle were. I put them on him, put the reins over his neck and said, "Come on." He followed me over to the sheep wagon.

Uncle Bob could only say, "I don't believe it!"

Croppy was a big, strong horse that I used every day. That let the other fellows use my two horses. Croppy loved to have me rope sheep off of him. I would take my rope down. It wouldn't matter what time of day it was. He would start prancing. Most of the time, it was from about seven in the morning until about eleven. That was the time when I was mothering up the ewes and lambs. He turned out to be one of the best horses I ever used.

I also had a dog. It belonged to Alberta's brother, Everett. He was part bulldog and part something else. Everett had some relatives in California and wanted to go out there. He didn't want to get rid of his dog, so he left him with me. I thought I could keep him at Uncle Bob's. There were three dogs at the ranch. They did not like to have a fourth. I didn't want to take him out with the sheep, because I thought that he would just be a nuisance. He was small and I felt sorry for the way the other dogs treated him. I finally took him along with me. I tied him up at the wagon. He was tied up there for two or three days. There were sheep all around. He really wanted to help, but I still wasn't sure of him.

One day I was trying to catch a week old lamb. That dog was giving every indication that he could do a lot better. I was so disgusted that I would try anything. I finally got mad enough to turn Doc loose. He just ran out and grabbed the lamb by the side of the neck. Since he was part bulldog, he could lock his jaw and nothing was going to throw him off. The lamb was big enough that he could swing Doc around in a circle. This allowed me to be able to get up to them. Why had I been so stupid? Doc could catch any sheep. It was a circus to see some large old ewe swinging around and around with that small bulldog hanging onto the side of her neck. That was the start of a real close relationship. That little dog might have weighed thirty five pounds. He would grab an old ewe by the side of the head and the merry go round would start.

To just have a dog around really gets the sheep's attention. Sheep have a lot of enemies, such as coyotes and wolves. Their only defense is awareness and speed. One of the things I liked about Doc, was that he would stay in one place when I told him to. I took him with me in the morning when I started pairing up the ewes and lambs. I would find a place which was quite a ways from the sheep. I would put an old glove, shoe or anything else down by Doc and tell him to stay, and he would. He was small enough so that he couldn't see me over the sagebrush. He would stand up on his hind feet to keep track of me while I was working with the sheep. The ewes would watch that crazy thing bobbing up and down and wouldn't pay any attention to me. Then I could get to them.

It was so wet and muddy that Doc looked like a drowned rat most of the time. Doc certainly wasn't a natural-born sheep dog, but he knew what I wanted and he liked to do it. He worked great for about a week then he decided to take a rest. He wouldn't go after a nasty old ewe one morning and I scolded him. He just went to the wagon and lied down. Finally, I said to him, "Doc, would you please consider catching that lamb?" It took me a week to get back in his good graces. From then on it was, "Would you mind coming with me this morning and catching some sheep?"

We lambed that 3,000 head of sheep in about three weeks. We had over 3,000 lambs that year. Uncle Bob said that it was the first time in eight years that he had over 100 percent lamb crop. We four young fellows felt that we were pretty special. We did a good job with the lambs that year, and I liked working with the sheep.

We had a nice little house there and enjoyed many things about the ranch. There was one thing that I did not enjoy. Aunt Janet had a little year old goat. If there was ever anything that I would have liked to stake to an ant hill, it was that goat. It climbed all over Aunt Janet's car. It jumped over the fence into where we had Glen. One day, Aunt Janet and Uncle Bob went some place and left the dinner dishes on the table. That little goat got in there and climbed all over the table. She knocked a dish of butter upside down on the wood floor. What a mess! To this day I do not know why that goat did not meet with a fatal accident.

The next spring, Glen had a severe attack of diarrhea, which we could not stop. We were many miles from a doctor and had no telephone. Even though I enjoyed being there and working with Uncle Bob, it was somewhat frightening for Alberta. We needed to get Glen to a doctor, so we decided to move back to Rapid City. I took Alberta and Glen there and went back to Uncle Bob's. A couple of fellows and I had decided to shear sheep. We started with Uncle Bob's. I worked at shearing until sometime in July.

About two years before we went to Uncle Bob's, I had filled out an application for a Civil Service job as a meat inspector. I had forgotten about it, since I had heard nothing. When I returned to Rapid City from the shearing, I received a notice on a Friday, that I was to be in Washington, D.C. a week from the following Monday to start work as a file clerk in the Veteran's Bureau. Since $1,200 a year was more than $40 a month, I thought that it was a good move. This was in the summer of 1941. I guess that I was under my lucky star. Since I was in the Veteran's service, I wasn't tapped to go into World War II. I didn't believe in volunteering, but if I had been called, I would have gone. I was in Washington D.C. just a year.

The military services were drafting the 17 to 19 year old boys. They didn't want to take the "old" men who had never been in the military service. They needed paper pushers and thought that anyone over 25 should be able to do that if they treated them well and did not overwork them. They didn't realize that most country bumpkins didn't know what a five day work week or an eight hour day was. There were about 20 of us to file the amount of papers that five could have done. My first reaction was, "What am I doing here?" I thought the authorities were expecting war and were getting ready for it

I was really amazed when I reported there for work. I had been used to working from daylight until dark, and had no break between meals. I went to the desk to get orders. The clerk found about a dozen papers to file. It took me about 15 minutes to file them. I went back to the desk for more work. I had noticed that nobody seemed to be in much of a hurry. The lady at the desk looked through a stack of papers and found a few more for me to file. She said, "That's all for now." I couldn't believe that I was getting paid for killing time. I was soon bored and didn't like it.

I got acquainted with a young man at the trailer camp. He was in charge of putting a very large steel culvert under the railroad track. I got to visiting with him. He said that if I wanted to work some at night, he could sure use me. It worked out that I could work six hours a night. I went home and slept for awhile and went to work at the Bureau. It didn't take me long to do my work there. There were some real wide window sills back of the file cabinets. I told one of the boys that if anyone was looking for me to just give me a buzz. I would go back there and sleep for an hour or two.

I was hired as a file clerk in the Veteran's Bureau. What we were dealing with was the records of all of the country's military men and women. There were thousands of young people leaving home at the same time. Every one was given a serial number that identified them. Few people realized that in all of this vast number of people, how many names, birth dates, states of birth, and other information were exactly the same. If we, as file clerks, had the serial number of the person, that was an exact identification.

There was a small place on the induction orders where it said to be sure to use the serial numbers when seeking information. A lot of parents or wives didn't realize how important that number was. The Veterans Bureau had a dead end file. You think that you get an unending bunch of mail for the waste basket! Every time I had to use that dead end file I really thought, "There has to be something missing here. How can there be so many unknown files? Why didn't someone tell people about the importance of the serial numbers?"

I finally got up enough courage to go to our boss and ask why there wasn't something done about making everyone more aware of the importance of that serial number. She said that was a good idea, but she couldn't do anything about it. I thought, "It doesn't end here." I went clear to the top secretary. Everyone was real nice until I got to the top. She said, "What can I do for you?"

I just told her my name. Boy, what a change that made! She said, "We know all about you. We don't need some country bumpkin telling us how to run our business. You better go back down and do your job."

At that time we had two choices if we were not satisfied in our job. We could transfer to another Veterans Bureau, or go into the army. I applied for a transfer to Denver. Within a week, I got it. I worked for the Veteran's Bureau there just a year. I decided to quit and work on a ranch in Delta, Colorado. One of the bosses told me that I couldn't quit the Civil Service at that time. However, as long as ranching was considered an essential industry, he could not do anything about it.

While we were on the ranch, about 12 miles from Delta, our second son, Larry, was born. We were busy haying. Our house was about a mile from the boss's house. I went home for dinner. Alberta said that I had better go get the boss's wife to take her into town. We had made arrangements with her earlier. I went down there and she asked me if I thought that she had time to do the dinner dishes and change her clothes. I told her that I thought it would be all right. She was a nurse, so she decided that she had better come right away.

They did not ordinarily take maternity cases at their little hospital in Delta. We had made arrangements with a lady who took them in her home. We picked up the doctor at his office and went to that house. The lady was not home. The doctor knew of another place so we went there. That house was full. The doctor said that we had better go to the hospital By that time, we had to carry Alberta up some long, steep stairs. They had just dismissed a patient, so they had a bed available. The nurse was just changing the sheets. I tried to hurry her. She took one look at Alberta and got her on the bed. The doctor had gone down stairs to wash his hands. The nurse said, "If you want to get in on this, you had better get up here." He handed me a can of ether and told me to sprinkle some when he told me. I gave Alberta a couple of whiffs and Larry was there. I went down town to get a couple of things for Alberta. Then

Glen, Larry, and I on Croppy

I caught a ride back to the ranch. In those days they kept maternity patients in the hospital for ten days. Grandma Ermish was taking care of Glen. When I got to the ranch, I put a new tongue in the hay rake and was ready for haying the next morning.

When I went over to that ranch, I had been told that I might get to manage it, because the manager was retiring. Instead, the ranch was sold to an Iowa man. He really did not know much about ranching in that part of the country. He made several bad mistakes.

We were living in a funny old frame house. It was set right out in the middle of the alfalfa field. We had rabbits and chickens. We had no bed for Larry, so he had to sleep on an old packing box. We had running water in the house, but no electricity. We had oil lamps and an old wood cooking stove. We had a little outhouse in back. We took our baths in the washtub. We washed all clothes by hand. We had two tubs. One was for washing and one for rinsing the clothes. Glen had watched Alberta put a little bluing in the rinse water. They did not have disposable diapers in those days. One day, when Alberta had a whole tub full of diapers in the rinse water, she went around the house to hang out something. While she was gone, Glen dumped the rest of the bluing into the rinse water. From then on, Larry wore blue diapers.

Alberta was nursing Larry. We had no car, so we did not get into town very often. Finally, we realized that Larry was just not doing very

54

well. We took him into the doctor. He said that he thought that he might have a brain tumor. One of his eye pupils was enlarged. He decided that we should take him to Colorado General Hospital in Denver. We called Grandma Ormesher. She met us in Denver. When the doctor examined Larry, he said that his "milk cow" had just petered out. We all went over to Chadron and I left the family with my Mom and went back to the ranch.

I knew that I had to find another job. They were scarce. I went up to Gunnison, Colorado. I had heard that someone needed a man to feed cattle. I went to work for an old German gentleman. He had about 100 head of cows to feed, but he didn't have a house where I could keep my family. Alberta and the boys went to Rapid to stay with her mother for the winter.

In the spring, I sent for Alberta and we rented a house in Gunnison. They stayed in town and I worked on the ranch. We didn't have a car. I got into town on Saturday evenings once in a while. The ranch had an old truck that we used for all purposes. It wasn't in the best of shape. We did drive it to Delta once in a while. I thought that some day it would be just my luck to get stopped. It wouldn't help matters if I didn't have a driver's license. I had to go to Delta, so it was time to get that license.

The brakes weren't too good on that old truck, but I thought that, if I had to take the driving part of the test, they might have a car that we could use. I parked the truck a couple of blocks away and walked to the license office.

I got the paper work done all right, but they wanted me to drive. The guy got his papers collected. We went out to the front of the building. There was a nice little Chevrolet coup parked along the street. With no hesitation, we proceeded to get into it. The key was in it. Naturally, I started it up and away we went. We were gone for fifteen or twenty minutes. Everything went fine. We came back to where we started. There was a sheriff and a young man standing on the sidewalk discussing who had stolen his Chevrolet.

The guy who tested me said that that was the first time that he ever got caught giving someone a driver's test in a stolen car. He thought that the car was mine and I thought that it was his.

The sheriff said, "Take my advice and don't make a habit of this." I was glad that I was not the guy giving the test. He was going to be around for a lot of razzing.

I still needed money. I had a pay check coming, but it wasn't in my pocket. We had a few belongings, but no place to put them. It was time to put up hay on the ranches and I knew that I could get a job stacking hay. In 1944 there was very little hay baled even in square bales. The round bales came much later.

I went to a pool hall to see if they knew of someone who needed a worker. They happened to know of a man who needed someone to help with the hay. His name was Douglas Spann. He needed full time help. He said that he had a cabin where we could live. It was about fifteen miles from Gunnison toward Crested Butte. I thought that maybe I could get out of a bind for awhile. I put our goods on a small truck and went to see the cabin. When we got there, the cabins turned out to be little, wood frame, one room shacks. We found the cabin a mess. It had an old, small cook stove, which had no oven door. The paper was coming off the wall. It didn't look like a place in which a family could live in the winter time. A ground hog would have refused to stay in one over the winter in that climate. We went back to Gunnison. Alberta looked at me and I could read her mind. I said, "No, we don't need to take this."

The lady looked at me and said, "I suppose that you would like to live in my house."

We went back to Gunnison. The fellow who had let me use his truck was wonderful. He let me leave our stuff on the truck until the next day.

The next morning I was at the employment office early. I sure hoped that they had a job waiting. Soon an elderly man came in. I was introduced to Mr. Lang Spann. Another Spann! Wow! Where was my luck? He had three boys and he was an uncle to Douglas Spann. Lang's son, Virgil, needed a man to help stack hay. He lived close to Gunnison. His dad said that Virgil had a house we could stay in. He said that it hadn't been used for awhile and might be dusty, but that it was a good house. I went out and looked things over before I said that I would take the job.

Virgil had an elderly man stacking hay. He didn't know a great deal about what he was doing. He was doing a poor job of keeping up. I started to help, and told the old gentleman that he was making twice the work out of the job than he should. It was hot. It was probably at least ninety degrees. I got sick. I would crawl off the stack, bathe my face and up-chuck if I could, and go back on the stack. I lasted out the day.

When I got to the house, I had to uncrate the mattress. We just laid it on the floor. That is where we all slept that night. The next morning I was feeling better. Those Spanns turned out to be real nice folks. I finished helping stack their hay. Then they gave me a choice of working for Virgil or his brother, Woodard. Woodard had a real nice three roomed cabin. He had just put new linoleum on the big main room. He said that he would get the paint if I wanted to repaint the indoors. The ranch was about fifteen miles from Gunnison toward Crested Butte. We moved up there and I helped finish Woodard's hay.

Having plenty of hay in reserve has always been a necessity in raising range cattle. This western country has been known for its severe snow storms when cattle could easily starve if not fed. By the year 1945, a lot of ranchers were using tractors with a seven foot sickle bar to cut the hay. After the hay was cut, it usually took three or four days for the hay to dry before it was raked into windrows. They used a side delivery rake to do this. The windrows were made so that the sweeps could pick it up. The sweeps had about seven foot long teeth made out of hard wood. They were sharpened on the front end so that they would go under the hay. The sweeps were pulled by two horses. When the driver got a load of hay from the windrow, he would take it and put it on the stacker and then back off. The stacker head was pulled up by two horses. When the stacker got straight up it hit blocks so it couldn't fall over. The hay slid off onto the stack. There were one or two men on the haystack with pitchforks to spread the hay around. The haystack always needed to be higher in the center, so that when it settled it would slant to the outside. Then the water would run off instead of going down into the hay. The men spreading the hay on the stack had to know how to move the hay fast. We let about three loads pile up. Then we could take our pitch forks and push the top load in different directions and as it slid down it pretty well spread out. It was a challenge to keep the sides straight as the stack got higher. Well stacked hay could last for six to eight years.

Haying time was a very busy time. When the hay was ready to be put up, every one wanted it put up right then. A week's time made a lot of difference in the second cutting. This was because of frost in the fall. If it was alfalfa hay, the frost could spoil the seed

Stacking hay gave way to bailing hay, first in small square bails and later in the large round bails.

The Spanns had a cow camp about five miles from the ranch. Woodard, his two brothers and their dad, took in hunters from out of town and acted as their guides. Hunting season lasted all of November. They had about twelve big horses. We had a great time hunting deer and elk.

It was a wonderful move for me. I loved hunting. Woodard took in hunters. Many of them couldn't hit a deer if we ran it over the top of them. We started hunting the first of November. The hunters paid for their license and for a deer or elk. It wasn't against the law to fill their license for them. We moved back to Nebraska when the season ended.

There was another thing that I greatly enjoyed there. The Gunnison River bordered the place. It had a lot of big trout in it. The irrigation ditches ran out of that river. When we shut the water out of the ditches in August, there were a lot of big trout in the ditches. If we left them in there over night, the mink and other animals would clean them out. So we had a lot of fun chasing them around and catching some of them. One time, Zilpha, Woodard's wife, and her children, Allen and Terry, were helping us catch fish. A nice big one went under a bridge. Zilpha went under there to chase it out the other side. All of a sudden there was a terrible noise under the bridge. A fish had gone up her pants leg. She nearly raised the bridge. I had fun getting Glen down in the ditch and chasing big fish up toward him. He was not always sure that he liked that. The irrigation ditches not only brought fish, they also brought hordes of mosquitoes. When I was irrigating, I had to cover all exposed parts of my body with netting, gloves, etc.

I really liked it there but I was only making a living wage and there was no way to get ahead. Alberta didn't feel very well. The doctors could find nothing wrong. She went back to Chadron for a visit and felt much better there. We decided that it was too high an altitude for her. It was 8,000 feet at Woodard's. Mom found us a job with Fred Wild on a ranch north of Chadron, so we moved back to Nebraska. Glen was in the second grade. Mrs. Wild was the teacher. Her son was in the eighth grade that year. There were not enough students to have school there the next year. There was no place for Glen to go to school. So we had to do something else. Alberta applied for a teaching job in Chadron. The only opening was in the first grade. She had never taught just first grade but she took it. I went to work in a filling station. I worked there for awhile then worked for a furniture store. We rented for awhile then bought a nice house in Kenwood. It was very close to the school. We paid $6,000 for it. We stayed there for one year.

BACK HOME

ALBERTA'S MOTHER WAS GETTING to the place where it was not safe for her to live alone. She was not willing to move out of her house. Alberta's brother talked us into moving in with her. We rented our house in Chadron and moved to Rapid City. Alberta got a job teaching first grade in Rapid. I went to work for Buckingham Wood Products building grain doors for $35 a week. We had bought an old Chevrolet just after World War II. It ran and that was all. It needed a new engine. We didn't have any money, so we walked to work. In about a year, I bought an old Buick. It burned more oil than gas, which was a lot. It cost two hundred dollars. I kept it about a year and traded it in on a used Chevrolet.

I worked for the Wood Products for about three weeks, and then went to work for the Coast to Coast Hardware store as a clerk. I liked that, but the pay wasn't much. I worked there about three years. Then I went to work at the Black Hills Power and Light Co. We took care of transformers and line materials. It was better pay and interesting work. I worked there until the upper crust got dissatisfied and was crabbing at everybody so I quit. I went to work for the Rose Marketeria grocery store.

The boys were in Cub Scouts. I took an active part in that. Then they were in Boy Scouts and we spent quite a bit of time at that. Both

of the boys went to National Jamboree. Glen went to California. Larry went to Valley Forge.

When Glen got into high school, he wasn't tall enough to be on the school basketball team. Some of the boys got together and had five teams that played against each other. I thought that they were pretty good. I tried to get the coaches to let the high school team play against Glen's team, but they wouldn't do it. I think that Glen's group could have beaten the high school team when they were seniors. They had played together for four years and they were really good.

I worked for the Rose Marketeria for two years. Then I bought a large van and put a refrigerator with a big freezing compartment in it. I called it the Handy Wagon. I delivered ice cream, bakery goods, pop and candy all over town. I went mostly to schools. Some of the elderly people really loved it. They wanted to keep me there to visit. It went fine for about a year. The Safeway Store came to town. I could buy ice cream from them cheaper than I could buy it wholesale. The kids got so pesky at school that it became a real headache. I decided to sell out after a year.

I went to work for Buckingham Transportation Co. I worked on the dock loading and unloading those big trucks. North Dakota was having a big oil boom. They were buying all kinds of equipment for that. They were also buying all kinds of farm machinery. They had load limits that were a lot less than South Dakota's. So when things came in here that were going to North Dakota, we had to reload a lot of stuff for them. We could work all the overtime we wanted. They told us to work at least 12 hours a day. Some days we put in 14 or 16 hours. We made good money, but we earned it. I worked for them for seven and a half years. One of the fellows who was a regular on the crew, was made foreman. It really went to his head. He had been well liked, but he really thought that he was a hot shot. It was not nearly as pleasant as it had been before. They finally let me go. The Union man said that there was no way they could do that if I wanted to fight it. I was ready to quit anyway.

I had decided that I wanted to start a ranch where I could help some high school kids in the summer. As usual, we didn't have any money. I took it to the church. Mary Lou Hermes' dad had just given his three kids $40,000 each and told them they could do what they wanted to do with it. I borrowed $3,000 from Mom and Bill. Together we bought

The Circle H Brand

what we called the Circle H Camp Ground. There were 211 acres in the place at the time. I built 75 camping sights and a shower house. We bought eight horses with riding equipment. At that time we could use high school students as guides. I started a riding school but got too busy to keep it going.

Later, I bought two horses at the sale ring in Rapid. One was a big, pretty, gentle sorrel. The other one was smaller but very wild. A man rode the sorrel horse into the ring. He said that he was well broken. They just turned the little horse into the ring and said that he was halter broken. When I went to get them, I stepped into the pen with the little horse. He just shook his head and started toward me. I didn't know what I had. I roped him and tied him on about ten feet of rope. I led him out of the gate and into the alley. The alley was covered with cement. He took off. When he hit the end of the rope, he really threw himself. He got up and came back to me. I finally petted him and got a halter on him. I led him up into the pickup with the big sorrel.

The next morning I saddled up the big sorrel expecting no trouble. I got on him and he threw me saddle and all. I had a double cinch on the saddle. I put the saddle back on him, got on and he threw me again. I took the back cinch off and really tightened up the other one. I took the horse into a small corral and got on him again. He couldn't get going very well in that small space but he sure tried. I had some logs to skid up for fire wood so the smart aleck got to be a work horse. I fastened the rope to the log and to the saddle horn and he pulled them for me. I rode him some. A young man from the air base also rode him. One day I needed to look at our cows and some others in another pasture. The country was real rough with canyons and hills. I rode that horse real hard and thought that he was pretty tired. I started out across the flat and that darned horse really went to bucking. I had a good saddle and I rode him until he almost reached a fence. He quit bucking. I loosened up a little and he whirled and I went off. I lit on my feet. He went a little ways down the fence and stopped. I caught him and walked with him to the corral. I took the saddle off. I told him that he didn't know it but he had just bought himself a new home.

A short time later, three young men came out. One of them asked if I had anything that would buck. It had rained the day before. One corner of the corral was quite high. The opposite corner had quite a puddle of mud in it. I told that young man that I had a horse that would buck but I didn't want to let him ride it because he might get hurt. He finally convinced me to let him try. I saddled the horse and led him up to the high spot. The young man got on and the horse just stood there. I asked him if he was ready. He said that he was. I just stepped back and slapped that old horse on the back end. He went about six feet in the air. When they came down the guy was on the back end of that horse. On the next jump they parted company. The guy landed right on his rear at the edge of that mud puddle. He made a good sled and looked a real mess. He wanted to try again. I told him no way. He didn't get hurt and I knew that there was no way that he could ride that horse. Several people wanted to ride him on trail rides, but of course we couldn't use him.

The Fourth of July came and our wranglers wanted to have a little celebration. They put on a show and to finish it off I saddled up the sorrel horse. I said to the campers, "Now I'll show you why we can't use him on the trail rides." I just stepped back and popped him on the back with my open hand. That old boy really put on an exhibition. A fellow came along with a gentle mare and traded for the sorrel. They put him in a bucking string, but I don't know where he went.

One of the wranglers went to riding the little wild horse. He gentled right down. I used him for roping. The wrangler started carrying kids on him. You just guess about a horse. They are like people. You can't always tell by the looks. We had the camp for four years. I liked it, but we had to insure our horses with Lloyds of London. That was expensive. We didn't have enough water, so we needed to dig another well. That would have been very expensive and there was no guarantee that you could get water. We decided to sell and we made a pretty good profit on it.

The Hermes and I went to Canada to look for a ranch. We found that the ranching in Canada wasn't as good as it was in the good old USA. The land was about the same price but the winters were longer and the roads to get to market were bad. We came back home. I located a small ranch 31 miles west of Belle Fourche. It wasn't big enough for two families, so I bought it.

I kept Norm's 15 head of cows and borrowed enough money from Uncle Bob to buy 500 head of sheep. I gave $10,000 to the realtor. This was supposed to go into an escrow account until I got an F.H.A. loan. He said that he would put it into the account. I told him that I would do it. He seemed like a nice guy so I let him talk me into letting him take care of it. He had drawn up a contract which stated that if the F.H.A. loan did not go through, I would get my money back. Instead, he took the $10,000 check, cashed it, took out his $3,000 commission and paid Carlson the other $7,000. Carlson was the ranch owner. He was a boozer and not dependable. I jumped all over the real estate dealer. I told him that he had better hope that the deal went through because there were going to be some people who would be sorry if it didn't. Of course, I knew that I might be able to put him in jail but that wouldn't bring my money back. To sue him would have been like suing a snow bank.

I was supposed to get the F.H.A. loan on September 3rd. It was March 3rd. when I finally got it. I took my papers to a lawyer in Rapid City to see what kind of contract I had. I did not know enough about legal papers. He told me to take it to Sundance, since that is where the business would be done. He gave me the name of a law firm there. I went to a lawyer there. He told me that my contract was no good and that he would have to draw up another one. I let him go ahead. When he got through he had about an eight page document. I was dumb enough to sign it. However, he had made the mistake of requiring my wife's signature, too. When I sat down and studied the papers, I discovered that it was all in Carlson's favor. I told Alberta that there was no way that she should sign it. She read it and agreed. I told those lawyers that I would not accept their contract. They sent me a bill for $60. I threw it in the waste paper basket. I got another rather nasty notice. In the meantime, I learned that one of the lawyers in the firm was representing Carlson. I got on the phone and got hold of the lawyer who had drawn up the contract. I told him that I had received two notices for bills for writing a contract which I would not accept. I did not want to hear any more about it. I heard no more. I finally accepted the one page contract which had been written up by the realtor.

I bought the ranch from a man who thought that beavers were a nuisance. They cut down trees and built dams where he didn't want them. He didn't know that by spreading the water out more trees could be watered. Beavers build dams out of logs and branches woven together. Then they fill in the cracks with grass and mud. Sometimes, water can flow over the dam. Usually, the dams are not washed out.

The ranch I bought, was in some hills in Wyoming. They called the area Bear Lodge. It joined the Forest Reserve, which was made up of higher hills. The creek, which came through the middle of the ranch, started in the higher hills. The beaver had built about 15 dams on about three miles of the creek. The owner blasted out the dams and killed all of the beaver on the ranch. Naturally, about the middle of June, the creek quit running.

The first thing I did when I moved onto the ranch was to cut quaking aspen trees and haul them to where the old dams had been. I started as close to the Forest Reserve as I could. Aspen trees are part of the beaver's favorite food. The wood is easy to cut and the beavers like to use it for their dams. The beavers have big, sharp front teeth. They live to be about 12 or 14 years old. They usually leave the family when they are two years old. Sometimes they go quite far away, but usually they just go for a ways up or down the same creek.

Shortly after I had put the aspen out near the old dams, I saw the couple of beaver that became the parents of my beaver family. From the first, they seemed to know that I was a friend. I could sit on a bank, not far from where they were working. They would come quite close to look at me. Sometimes it seemed as if they wanted to say, "Why don't you come in and take a swim?" The first summer, when they had started to rebuild the dams, they had their first family of three baby beavers. I had fun watching them.

Having water around, like the beaver dams, puts more water into the air through evaporation so that more rain falls. My beaver family helped me with my ranch, because they made water available for my sheep and cows in the hot summer. I didn't have to build a dam or pump water from a well. When I sold the ranch I really missed my beaver family.

Not long after I got the ranch, I bought 226 head of sheep at the sale barn at Belle Fourche. I didn't have any money, but I was going up to Uncle Bob's to see if I could borrow enough to buy 500 head. The sheep looked real good to me. I thought that if I could buy them for $15 a head, they would be worth it. They didn't come into the ring until after six o'clock that night. One other person thought the same thing I did. I bid $14.75. He bid $15. I thought I would give him one more chance. I said $15.50 and got the sheep. I thought if worse came to worst, I could leave them there that week and sell them the next. I went up to Uncle Bob's and he said we could go down and look at them. When he saw them, he said that there were eleven old ewes that I should cut back and sell. Otherwise they were worth the money. I was pleased and it turned out that they saved my hide. Two days before Thanksgiving, I went out east of Belle Fourche and bought enough sheep to make up the 500. The day before Thanksgiving I got a truck to haul them to the ranch. It started snowing and I asked the truck driver if he had chains. He said that he wouldn't need them.

We got to one of the worst hills about four o'clock. It was snowing and getting dark. The truck got almost to the top of the hill and spun out. Back down the hill we went. The back of the truck ran up on the bank. The truck teetered back and forth. I thought sure that it was going over. It finally settled right side up. A neighbor came along and took me up the road a ways to get a caterpillar tractor to pull the truck up the hill. There was another hill about a mile up the road. The tractor pulled the truck up that hill. It wasn't too far to a ranch. The young fellow on it said that I could put my sheep in his corrals for that night. On Thanksgiving morning I got my horse and drove the sheep on home. It was about six miles.

I had some hay for that winter and I bought some more. I also bought a small amount of cake. Altogether, I fed about 25 tons of hay. A cow is supposed to need as much hay as five head of sheep. I had 15 head of cows and 500 head of sheep. My neighbor had 100 head of cows. The next spring, he asked me how much hay I had fed. I told him that I had fed 25 ton. He said that he fed his cows over 125 tons of hay and could have used more.

During the summer, I had a young man working for me. He had been with us when we had the camp grounds. His name was Jim Rhinebold. Our older son, Glen, had two boys, Larry and Steven. They stayed with Jim and I that summer. We were batching it and really having a good time. There was a frog pond close to the trailer. It was just right for two boys to go swimming and rafting. It was great for catching frogs and pollywogs. Sometimes there were even garter snakes.

One day I had Larry, the older one, with me on a mowing machine cutting hay. A little fawn jumped up in the grass. We had our little Sheltie dog, Laddie, with us. Larry jumped off the mower and he and the dog took after the deer. They ran it up into some timber. It hung up on a log and Larry caught it. The little deer started kicking. Larry had quite a time, but he finally turned its feet away from him. He came carrying it down to where I was. He shouted, "I got him, Grandpa. I got him."

We got on the tractor and went up to where Jim and Steve were raking hay. The boys were both very excited and thought that the little deer was very nice. They wanted to keep it. I asked, "What will you feed it? We don't have any milk."

They had an answer, "The cow has a calf. You can rope the cow, and get some milk." That was a good thought, but I was afraid that the cow would not agree. The next problem was what the mama deer would do without her baby. The boys thought it over for awhile. They really wanted to pet the little deer. I told them that they shouldn't handle the little deer any more than they had to, because the mama deer wouldn't like our smell on her baby. They hadn't realized that all animals have their own scent.

"What is scent?" they asked.

"Oh, just smell. Now it is time to take the little deer back and turn it loose up in the timber where its mother will find it. That little deer can brag that a couple of little boys patted it."

The baby deer was really frightened, but they had not hurt it. It made strange noises. It sure would be glad to see its mother again.

That was very exciting, but it was just one of several experiences with animals for the boys. It was not very long after that when we cornered a big raccoon in the granary. There were two open windows in the granary; one on each end of the building. Jim got up to one window with a stick, and I got up to the other with a stick. If that old coon tried to come out, we would whack him on the nose. There were some cracks in the building, so that the boys could see that coon climbing around.

We didn't want to kill the coon, but we didn't really know what we were going to do with him. Finally I fixed the board shutter on the window, so that the coon could not get out. I had the big dog at the time. Both dogs wanted to get in on the action. I opened the door and the big dog dashed in. There was a terrible racket. I opened the door again and a tangle of dog and coon came piling out. Then the coon got loose and he sure lit out for the trees.

We had some very excited boys. "Grandpa!" said Larry, "Boy that old coon sure was a scrapper. Weren't you afraid that he might take you on even if you had a stick? I sure wouldn't want to try to stop him!"

Needless to say, we didn't see that old coon again. I am not sure that the big dog would have welcomed him back.

I had sheared plenty of sheep before, so that first spring, I decided to shear my own sheep. When I was younger and shearing sheep with Dad, I could shear one hundred sheep a day. I found that it was like being an athlete. Without practice, your muscles forgot what they were supposed to do and got weak. The years since my shearing days were telling. I thought the shearing would last all summer!

Alberta stayed in town. Her mother was in a wheel chair a lot of the time. She could not be left alone for long periods of time. Of course,

Alberta was teaching school in the winter. On the sixth of March I went to Rapid. I had not been down for about two weeks. It was snowing, but I fed the stock well and decided that the storm would not last long. I went to Rapid and it continued to snow all night, all the next night, and all the next day. It was a little better the third day, which was Sunday. I waited until Monday morning.

I thought that maybe the roads would be cleared enough so that I could get back to the ranch. The stock had to be fed, if I had any left. I made it fine until I got to the turn off four miles west of Aladdin. I only had 11 more miles to go. The snow cover was anywhere from bare ground to 15 feet deep. I stopped on the road wondering what in the world I could possibly do. I just sat there for about 10 minutes. Then my old friend came along with his caterpillar tractor to clear out the road. It was about a mile over to the nearest ranch. I waited until he had dozed the road that far and then drove my truck that far. The rancher said that I had just as well stay for dinner because I sure couldn't get up to the ranch. Just after dinner, a neighbor who lived about two miles from my place came down with a four wheel drive log skidder. He was going over to the highway to get some gas for the skidder. I sure was glad to see him. When he came back I caught a ride with him. I left my truck there at the ranch. I got to about within a mile of my place and the snow was so deep that the skidder couldn't go through. The snow was crusted and I could walk on top of it so I started walking.

The snow drifted over the fences in a lot of places. About half of my sheep got up into the timber and kept tramping the snow down. One ewe was under the drifted snow so I lost her in that bunch. My saddle horse, the cows and all but three of the other sheep had gone to the sheds by the trailer. I caught my saddle horse. I had the hood from an old car. I tied my saddle rope to it. I loaded six square bales of hay and two sacks of cake on it and fed the first bunch of sheep. Then I did the same with the other bunch. Then I built fence on top of fence and snow drifts so the sheep couldn't get out. The three sheep that were drifted under and a ewe that laid down right by the shed door got drifted over and I did not find them until the snow melted. I was very lucky. A fellow who lived about eight miles from me lost 180 head. I didn't get my truck for two weeks. The horse I was using was the little wild one that I had at the Circle H Camp.

The second spring I had a friend and a fellow from Belle Fourche come and shear my sheep. I didn't feel like taking all summer to do it.

I made arrangements with the neighbor who had the logging skidder to cut some logs on my place. I had a saw and I had been cutting a few when I finished haying. About the first of January, I had been cutting some every day. Friday, the thirteenth of January was a cold, blustery day. I knew better than to cut timber on a day like that when the wind was blowing in every direction. It needed to be done so I went to cutting timber. When I started to cut down a tree, I noticed that it was going to lodge in one below. I went and cut that one down and started to trim it. The wind caught the one up above and snapped it off. Because of the noise of the wind and my saw, I didn't hear the tree break loose. I was far enough away, so only the branches hit me. They caught me on the head and back and knocked me away from the main tree. Luckily for me, the neighbor's boy had just come up with his jeep to clear a place to stack logs. I called to him and told him that I was in trouble. It was about a mile to my trailer and there was about a foot of snow. He brought his jeep up and took me to the trailer. He went home to get his dad's car to take me to the hospital in Belle Fourche.

I had about all I could take by the time we got to the hospital. I just collapsed into a chair in the waiting lounge. Some one grabbed a nurse and she wheeled me into the x-ray room. They found that I had two compacted vertebrae in one place and one in another. It was lower down in my back. The old doctor didn't want anything to do with me. He called for a specialist in Rapid City. Both bone doctors were out of town. On Saturday morning, he straightened me up and put a cast on me from my neck down as low as he could go and still let me walk. He kept me in the hospital for a week. Dr. Blunck, one of the specialists from Rapid was a friend of ours. When he got back to Rapid, he came right up to see me. He looked at the x-rays, used his mallet and spurs to see if I had any nerve damage. He said, "Son, you are very lucky. The old boy did as good a job as I could have done." I don't know whether Friday the thirteenth is lucky or unlucky. For me, it was a very lucky day.

The neighbors took care of the stock until the first of March. Then I took over again still wearing the cast. I wore it until the 15th of May. It got to smelling so bad that I couldn't go home. The doctor put me in a steel brace that I could take off and put on. I wore the thing until fall. I have had no trouble with my back since.

I missed out on Larry's and Shirley's wedding, which was on January 21st in Broomfield, Colorado. Alberta had to represent us both.

I stayed at the ranch that summer. Alberta had been accepted to go to DeKalb, Illinois to get her master's degree in elementary counseling. She needed to go in June to do some preparatory work. I took her and her mother there. Steve and young Larry stayed with Rose and Lloyd until I got back. I told Alberta that if she was going to be there all winter so was I. The boys and I kept the ranch that summer. I had to sell all the livestock so I could spend the winter in DeKalb.

I had already sold Norman Hermes' cows. I had to wait until my lambs were old enough, then I planned to sell my sheep. I had to separate the sheep because I had to know what ages they were and how I wanted to sell them. The weather doesn't seem to care what ranchers order. It started raining five days before the sale date. I waited for a break in the weather. I didn't get one. I had to start separating about 900 sheep with only my faithful Laddie for help.

Anyone who has handled sheep knows that a good dog can do more with sheep than two men can. My mother had two Shetland Sheep dogs. They were born and bred in Scotland for handling sheep. They also made good pets. They were imported into the United States. My mother knew that I could sure use one. She bought a small pup. I wondered if he would ever be anything but a toy. He was very little. She left him with Alberta in Rapid City. His full registered name was Wee Lad of Beaver Valley. We called him Laddie.

When Laddie was about two months old, Alberta brought him to the ranch for me. Alberta had not really seen the ranch, so I was taking her around. Laddie was slowly following along behind. We were not paying much attention to him. We came to a gate in a wire fence. I opened it to let Alberta through, then I shut it. The wire fence was high enough for the puppy to walk under it easily, but when he came to the gate, he just sat down and whined, as if to say, "You sure are inconsiderate." I had to go back and open the gate for him, too.

From the very first, I would carry him around and he really took an interest. He would lean down and growl and bark once in awhile and really get excited. It wasn't long until I had him on a leash and he was a great help. The biggest problem that I had with him was that he wanted to be with me all of the time. He couldn't stand it unless he was where the action was. He was very sensitive and really tried to understand what I wanted of him. He had his limits, but he sure knew that he could move sheep faster than I could. I had a big corral. When I had to have a big bunch of sheep in it and needed to separate some out for one reason or another, I had to tie Laddie on a long rope in the back of the corral so that he could move back and forth to keep the sheep moving through the cutting chute.

With all that rain, my corrals were a real mess. I had Laddie on his long rope. He was moving back and forth in that mud. Needless to say, he looked like a muddy, drowned rat. It took me two days. Laddie kept those sheep coming through the chute until the last one. We were both tired and didn't look like much, but I wanted to get started.

My friend, Lloyd Smith, had taken two of the mares that I had at the Circle H Camp Ground. One of them had an appaloosa colt. I asked him about taking it with me to DeKalb. He said that it would be fine. He didn't need him. I thought that there might be a pretty good market for him there. I had a pickup with a stock rack on it so there would be no problem.

I got to DeKalb about 11:00 at night. I had been there in June and I thought that I could locate Alberta's apartment. There had been some building going on in that vicinity that summer. They had built some more apartment buildings and planted sod on the lawns. There were a lot of sorority and fraternity houses around the apartment house where she lived. I arrived in the middle of the night. It was dark and rainy. I couldn't find the right place. Laddie and I slept in the truck that night. We knocked on the door about six the next morning.

Laddie and me

I didn't know whether Alberta would claim a wet rancher and his wet dog from the far reaches of Wyoming or not. Having been married to me for as long as she had, she was pretty hard to surprise, but she wasn't immune from surprises. I didn't tell her about the horse for awhile. That sort of took her breath away. Fortunately, she had made a friend whose family was living on a place in the country. She called him and asked if there was a place there where we could leave the horse until we found a place for him. He managed to find a location for him. The people at the University had a lot of fun over my horse. Later, I found a pasture where I could board my horse with about ten other horses.

LADDIE AND I

On a Sunday noon in April, we were eating dinner when the door bell rang. I went to the door. There was a real large man there and he looked angry. He said, "What are you going to do about that knot headed horse of yours breeding my mares?"

It surprised me but I said, "Wait a minute. I didn't think that it was time for that sort of business, but if anybody is going to get a colt out of that 'knot head' they are going to pay for it. His granddaddy was a $5000 show horse and his daddy sold for $3000 when he was a yearling. I don't have papers on that 'knot head', but I can get them. I sure am glad to find out what is happening. I would be glad to pen my horse up."

I asked the man if he was going back to the barns. He said he would and I told him that as soon as I finished dinner I would be down and talk some more. In about an hour I went down there. He had taken his mares and left. I guess he had second thoughts about my horse and his business.

I had several different occupations while we were in DeKalb. I worked at building big overseas packing crates for awhile. Then I worked at drying DeKalb seed corn. When that was finished, I worked for a Del Monte canning company. Mostly, I painted 110,000 feet of steel frames that held up the building. In the spring we cleaned and greased machinery. They wanted me to stay there. They said that I would get a raise and could put in all the over time that I liked when they started canning. However, Alberta got out of school and of course we were headed back to South Dakota. I would have liked the job and the pay, but not Illinois. I would much rather spend my time at the ranch with Laddie.

As Laddie grew, he became a lot of help to me. He learned to help with the cows and the sheep. Best of all though, he was a wonderful companion. He went with me everywhere. When I sat down, he sat and studied me, trying to decide what I might want him to do next. He was very sensitive and I never dared to scold him. He was always doing his best.

The next fall, our son came home from Chicago, where he had been staying with his brother's family. He brought with him a very large dog. He had acquired it as a small puppy. It was in a box with others in a grocery store. A family was giving them away. He had owned a dog, which he had greatly loved. It was no longer living, and he could not resist this puppy. It grew rapidly. It had a very loving nature, and thought that it was a lap dog. Alberta was amazed when she saw the size of the dog. She told Larry that he had to take it with him. He was going back to Laramie to school. Knowing his tender hearted mom, he slipped away without him. There was no way that he could have that huge dog at school. Alberta was very happy to see me come home the next day. She knew that I would take the dog to the ranch.

That dog thought that everything was a plaything for him. The first thing he did, when I got him to the ranch, was to run up to a cow expecting her to run. She just turned and sent him rolling. Boy, she sure played rough! He decided that he would rather play with Laddie. About all that Laddie would do was to get out of his way.

I had him around for about six months. The only thing he was good for was to chase deer. I had to keep him tied up. He could get himself in the way, and do the wrong thing, every time I tried to do anything with the sheep or cows. He was the only dog I was ever around, that didn't take anything seriously.

I finally decided that I had to get rid of him. If I let him loose, he would go find himself a deer to chase. I was afraid that Laddie would finally think that maybe the chase was worth exploring. I did not want him chasing deer.

I contacted a kennel near Black Hawk. At that time they were very good at placing animals in homes. After I told them how friendly the clown was, and that he loved to play, they decided to take him.

When I got back to the ranch, Laddie seemed to miss the big dog. I had not thought how he might feel. For a month, Laddie would look at me and act like he thought, "Am I going to be next?"

He seemed to sense my every mood. Most of the time, when we were working with the animals, he appeared to know what should be done before I told him. He could do more with sheep and cattle than two men could. He was priceless as far as my work was concerned. How lucky I was to have a ranch and such a dog to help me. He also did an outstanding job of playing ball with me and my two grandsons.

When our oldest grandson, Larry, was seven years old, he was fascinated with the sheep, almost as much as Laddie. He wanted to buy a sheep. His dad said, "You'll have to deal with Grandpa about that, but you'll have to pay for it."

That made me do some thinking. What could I do to give a seven year old boy a job to earn some money?

We had a milk cow that had to be brought in every night. We had two dogs that had to be fed and watered. The dogs weren't allowed in the house, so feed and water took care of them. The sheep were in the pasture and didn't need any feed. However, we did have five bum lambs. A bum lamb is one that has lost its mother, or is rejected by her. A ewe can often have twins and may only claim one. Or, she may only have one, but will refuse to claim it in spite of all of the persuasion she will get. The first step to take in getting a sheep to take a lamb, is to expose her to several lambs to see if she takes an interest in one of them. If she does, you catch her and the lamb and put them in a small pen or tent. Or, you may take a short rope and tie it to one of her feet and stake her to a pin or sage brush. Then take a lamb and let it get its meal from a usually well supplied table. If you do this about three times a day, the ewe will usually claim the lamb. Of course, if you have a dog to help out, it can be the deciding factor. The threat of the dog seems to bring out the mothering instinct.

Taking care of five bum lambs can be quite a chore. That seemed like something that Larry might help with to earn his money. Do you go to the store and buy five bottles of milk? No, it is not quite that simple.

The milk comes from a cow or two. There are bottles to be washed and filled. Feeding the lambs is not simple either. The lambs fight to see which will be first. They sure do a good job of bunting the bottle. They never learn that bunting a bottle isn't nature's way of producing milk.

Larry got the lamb that he picked, and, of course, he had some help with his lamb feeding. That fall, I asked him if he would like to sell his lamb and buy another ewe. That took some thinking. I told him that the lamb was worth about the same as a ewe. In the spring, his ewe would probably have a lamb, then he would have two sheep. He would be in school in Denver and wouldn't get to see his lamb very often anyway.

He picked out a brown nosed ewe, so that he could tell it from the rest. However, he had me put a special mark on her, anyway. In the spring, his ewe had twins. He was really in the sheep business. That fall I sold the ranch, so Larry and I went out of the sheep business.

Our son, Larry, was drafted and ended up in Vietnam during the spring of 1968. His wife Shirley was expecting their first child. She was in Lake Charles, Louisiana. Larry had asked if we would go down to be with her for this occasion. Her mother was going to summer school and would not be available right away. We had agreed. Alberta's mother had consented to go into a nursing home. We took our tent and Laddie. We started on July third. Shirley called just as we were leaving. She had just been to the doctor and he had told her that the baby would probably arrive about the 16th. She told us to take our time. We had a wonderful time sight seeing on the way down. We arrived on the morning of the eighth day of July, only to be told that David had arrived the day before. We took them home the next day and stayed for about two weeks. In September, Shirley and David came to stay with us until Larry could get back home.

I took a job as janitor at Steven's High School. I worked there for two and a half years. Then Glen and I started a bicycle repair shop. Helping the boys through college had taken most of our money, so we really did not have enough to launch a business. The bicycle shop wound up to be a losing proposition. Again, I was in need of another job.

Just before the flood on June 9, 1972, Alberta and I had been spending a work day at Storm Mountain, the United Methodist Camp. One of the fellows there, Roger Harris, had been doing some road work. I asked him for a job. That was on Thursday. I was supposed to go to work on Monday. On Friday night we had a cloudburst. It rained about 14 inches in two hours. Rapid creek flooded and washed out Canyon Lake dam. It washed out many homes and 234 people died. Roger had been going up and down Rapid Creek trying to get people out of their homes. He was in a jeep and he started back up the road to see about his family. He had sent them up on a hill out of danger. Suddenly, a large piece of the road he was on broke off and floated down the valley. He jumped out of his car and tried to swim. He drowned. Had he stayed with his car he would have been all right. The jeep stayed on the piece of asphalt and lodged against some trees. Of course, it was so dark that you could not see anything that was happening.

The evening of the ninth, Alberta and I went across the street to Mellgren's and played cards for awhile. We knew that it was raining real hard but thought nothing of it. It let up a little and we scooted home. We didn't turn on the radio or TV, but went straight to bed. Edith and Mina planned to leave for Spokane early the next morning. Alberta had invited them to come over for breakfast before they left. Alberta got up about five o'clock and turned on the radio. She called to me and said, "You should come out here and hear what is happening." We couldn't believe that we slept through the whole mess.

The city had a large auditorium where they were gathering people. Those in charge were looking for homes to take in some of the people until they could go back to their own home, if they still had one, or make some other arrangements. I went down there and it was like those people were on an island and they weren't getting off. A lady was taking names, so that relatives, friends and authorities could locate people. I told her that we would be glad to have a family stay with us until they could get straightened out. Finally, she convinced a Mexican family, who had three little kids, they would be better off to go with me than to stay there. There were not enough bathroom facilities and there would not be anything to eat for some time. They stayed with us until that afternoon when some friends came and got them.

Car motors made cars heavier on the front than in the back. There were many cars standing on their front ends when the water went down. It looked funny to see a car with the back end against a telephone pole as far up as it could go and with the front wheels on either side of the pole

Cars during the 1972 flood - USGS file photo

with the front bumper buried in the mud right against the pole. There were probably 25 cars that way against the side of the dock at the mill.

One couple lived near the creek. It was raining when they came home. They drove into their garage. They drove into water, so they backed up. The big wall of water hit them and raised their car up. It raised it high enough so that it lodged on a picket fence. They stayed that way for about an hour. Some National Guard men found them and rescued them.

There was a high school band here from Germany. There were two brothers. The young people stayed in different homes around town. The creek washed through Haggerty's, a local department store. One of the brothers had been rescued there. They were drying him off with some of the store towels. The people stranded there had made a human chain extending out into the water trying to catch some of the people floating by. They brought one youngster in. All of a sudden he discovered his German brother. That was an exciting reunion. All the last boy could say was, "Haus kaput! Haus kaput!"

On Sunday morning, Mayor Don Barnett was at the Auditorium calling for heavy machinery operators and people to work on trucks clearing trash and looking for people. I went down to see what I could do. Don said that he didn't need any machinery operators right then, but if I wanted to I could take ten men and go over to a low lying trailer court and go through the trailers to see if there were any people in them. I took the ten men over there. I put two together and started them going through the trailers. Two of them went to a big pile of debris on the side of the bank. They were there about five minutes when one lifted up a rubber tire. There was a whistling noise. He shouted down to me, "Hey! There's a propane tank leaking, what shall I do?"

I said, "There had better not be any one around there smoking! I'll call the gas company." It only took a few minutes to get to a telephone, but by the time I got back, I didn't have a single man. The gas company got there right away and capped the tank.

A short time later, Bill Clason brought his big loader and bulldozer down and we started pulling the trailers out that would still hold together. Some were so filled with mud that they just dozed them into piles, loaded them on a truck and hauled them to the dump. Others floated pretty well and had varying amounts of damage. One was right next to a big cotton wood tree. The tree didn't have any limbs for up about thirty feet. It was right against the middle of the trailer. The trailer floated up and down the tree. It got about two inches of water in it. There was a TV on a small stand in the trailer. It was still sitting there undisturbed. About all the trailer needed was a new carpet and to be dried out.

I went to work on a regular basis because the company had been Harris and Clason before Roger was drowned. Roger's dad had been with Clason before Roger took his place. After Roger was drowned, his dad took back Roger's part of the company. They were together for about a year when Bill bought Mr. Harris out. The company was then Clason and Son's. For the most part we built small roads around Rapid City.

We did rebuild Highway 73, going north from Philip, South Dakota. There were nine miles of road and it took 73 culverts and one bridge. I had fun on that job. Most of the time, I fueled the equipment. I had as many as 32 big engines to refuel. There were tractors, scrapers, road graders and trucks. It took me about two hours twice a day. In between, I worked on the culverts or strung pipe to bring water for the road. The water came from an artesian well and it was hot.

One day I was working with the fellow who was acting foreman of this particular job. He was a small fast moving pepper pot. His name was Warren. Some of the fellows didn't get along with him, but for me, he was fun. One day I was working on a culvert. He drove up and said, "Come with me. We have a leak in the pipe-line."

We went to a place between two hills where the pipes had come slightly apart. We went to the well head and shut the water off and went back to fix the pipe. There was a coupling on each side of the pipe and one broke. The water was still coming out of the pipe. We had to get the side loose that was still holding. I put my bar under the pipe and was gently moving it so that I could get it back together to release the side that was still holding. I was too slow. Warren stuck his bar under the pipe and I backed out of the way. Warren gave the pipe a tug and the coupling broke, letting the pipe slide sideways so that water was coming from both sides. It made a beautiful shower!

It really sprayed Warren. He came out of there fast! He said, "Wow! That water really is hot!" I laughed at him and said that I thought maybe it was. We waited for about ten minutes for the pipe to drain.

Later, we were taking out some old culverts. We had put a big long pipe on the front of one of the big tractors so that we could run it into the culverts and lift them out of the way. The driver of the tractor started to lift two sections of the culverts. They were about three fourths full of dirt. Some way, the culverts spread apart far enough so that two large skunks dropped down. Their tails caught between the culverts. The driver shouted, "What shall I do now?"

There were four of us on the ground. As we were leaving, I shouted back, "That's your problem."

He eased the tractor out quite a ways. Then he shook the culverts up and down gently. It spread the culverts far enough so that the skunks could drop out. Believe it or not, those skunks scampered off without a bit of smell. We had a lot of fun kidding the skunk tamer.

Warren couldn't get along with the road inspector. We were working a big fill over a large culvert. Warren had been having trouble with the inspector because the inspector wanted the dirt real wet to put in the fill. We were working a ways away from the fill on the culvert. Warren got two scraper loads of dirt from the fill to put on the culvert.

The inspector came down and said the dirt was too dry. Warren was standing on the culvert. He threw his hat down and stomped on it. I thought maybe he was going to put the inspector in the fill. He said, "I just hauled that dirt down from the fill where you said that it was too wet! Now you say that it is too dry! You are the most obnoxious person I ever worked for!" He got in his pickup and roared off up the road.

I went ahead working on the culvert. In about five minutes, Warren came back and said, "Get in here." I got in his pickup and we drove up the road. He said, "I swear every morning that I won't get mad at that S.O.B., but he can sure find more ways to get my dander up!" We drove around for about thirty minutes then went back to work. As far as I know Warren never spoke to that inspector again. They communicated through the road surveyor.

I got in a lot of over time. While we were working on the road north of Philip, I had fun fishing on a lake just east of town. I took a big inner tube and put plywood on the bottom. Then I wrapped a waterproof tarp around it. It made quite a pontoon. I floated around on it and the fish were not at all afraid of it. I could catch a lot more fish than I knew what to do with so I turned them back.

One day Alberta and Glen's three children, Larry, Steven, and Carlin came down to spend the day with me. They spent part of the day under a bridge catching sunfish. They could get them alright so they thought that was fun. They had dinner with me in the evening. Then I took them to the lake. The water was too warm and the big trout were coming to the surface. We had a small, one man raft. Steven got on it and paddled around close to the shore. He was trying to hit the fish with a little plastic bat. Larry and I were running along the shore trying to snare a fish with a big hook. We didn't succeed but we sure had fun chasing the fish around. Carlin was running around squealing and trying to keep up.

The Park people said that they might have to move the fish because they were running out of oxygen. The wind came up and it rained so the water was better and the fish survived all right.

After we finished at Philip, we came back and worked around the Black Hills building forest service roads and county roads into housing projects. I never drove a scraper, but I did everything else. I liked to drive the small cat and finish around the culverts and finish off the roads. Most of the fellows didn't like that because it was painstaking and it involved cleaning up after the big monsters. I would have worked longer, but after age 65, I would have been working some of the time for the government. I would rather go fishing or traveling or just mowing the lawn. At least it was better for me. I worked for Bill Clason for seven and a half years. Then I retired. I never worked for a nicer fellow.

During those last few years we kept in touch with one of Alberta's childhood friends. Her mother had adopted Alberta and I as one of hers and with us came our family. She had lost all of her close family. She had a cabin off Highway 385 west of Rapid. She invited us to spend time with her at the cabin. We wound up spending the summers at the cabin after we sold the ranch. Our grandsons loved to visit us there. She loved children and since she didn't have any grandchildren, she adopted ours.

There were chipmunks, squirrels, raccoons, and birds that did a good job of being pets, or in some cases, pests. The chipmunks furnished the most entertainment. They got so tame that they would take peanuts out of our grandsons' hands or shirt pockets.

The feeders were supposed to be for the birds. That turned out to be a big problem. Chipmunks, squirrels, and raccoons are pretty resourceful animals. They all have a wonderful sense of balance and an ability to climb. They are all fond of bird seed. Chipmunks and squirrels live where there is timber. Coons like a place that is close to a stream or pond. The cabin was near all of them. It taxed my thinking to come up with something that would feed the birds, because the animals could clean up a lot of feed in one night.

At the cabin with David

I started out with a feeder on top of a post. That just lasted one night. I decided that if I put the feeder on top of a two inch pipe it would keep the raccoon from climbing it. I underestimated the coon's ability. Now, what would I do next? I had two young helpers. Grandpa surely would come up with some way to feed all of the animals and birds. It just takes time. I put a still smaller pipe under the feeder. Then I got a piece of stove pipe and attached it to the feeder over the small pipe. It swung free, so there was nothing for my friends to grab on to. The birds could eat at their leisure. The chipmunks had good care. The squirrels and coons could just find some other person's feeder.

RETIREMENT AND REFLECTION

ONCE I RETIRED, I had time to think about my life and how small the world had become.

I was born on a homestead in Montana and for ten years our family lived on that homestead. I would stand on the state line and look as far into Wyoming as the eye could see, and look north into Montana. The land looked the same. It looked very big to me. I wondered how big the United States was. We didn't know what electricity was. I had never heard about a telephone. We carried water from the creek in pails or used a horse and sled to haul it in barrels. Our post-master got the first car in our area. It was a model T Ford touring car. I am sure that it would go at the terrible speed of thirty miles an hour.

When we moved to Hot Springs, I saw several different kinds of cars, some telephones and running water. When I was 16, a man came to Hot Springs with a single wing, 85 horse power, two seater airplane. I was so excited. I decided that I had to have a ride in it. It was during the depression and I didn't have any money. So the pennies, nickels, and dimes were really horded. It cost a whole $3 for a five minute ride. I was afraid that the airplane would disappear before I could get my ride. The man stayed there for about a week and I got to be a bird. What a thrill that was.

My world was getting bigger. Then I went to Chadron State Teachers College in Chadron, Nebraska, where I met my future wife. It was quite a while before we moved to Rapid City. That was the big city then.

We bought a three quarter ton Chevrolet pickup with a big camper on it and we did quite a bit of traveling. We made several trips to the west coast. Shirley, David and Michael, and Carlin went with us at different times. On one trip we threw the rubber off a back tire. We thought the whole camper was flying apart, but when the rubber was all off the wheel turned as smoothly as before. We got into the next town where we got a new tire.

We took one special trip to Mountlake Terrace, Washington to see Everett and his wife Velma. Larry let us take his Cadillac car. He thought that we would be safer in a larger car. Alberta and I took Carlin, David, and Michael on the trip all by ourselves. Carlin had had an assignment in one of her classes to plan all expenses for a trip just like this. She probably had our trip in mind when she planned the paper. We got an AAA trip book and let David and Carlin choose our motels. They were told to choose two to four star places. We could hear them planning in the back seat. If the motel did not have a heated swimming pool, it was rejected. When we got back, we compared our actual expenses with those projected in Carlin's paper, they were very close.

We usually started about six in the morning and planned to stop by three or four in the afternoon. One of the places we really enjoyed was the sand dunes along the highway in Oregon. They were high and steep. The kids looked like sand dunes themselves when they got through rolling and burrowing in the sand. We all had a glorious time.

Alberta's brother, Everett, loved to go salmon fishing in the ocean. One time, Everett, Alberta, David, and I went on a fishing boat. We had a real nice young fellow for a captain. He took very special care of David as he was pretty small. Along in the afternoon, I caught a good sized salmon. I was up in the bow of the boat and usually everyone would roll in their lines when someone had a fish. One stupid character had to leave his line out. The fish was about to tangle our lines and the captain reached up to cut the other fellow's line. He cut the wrong one. I knew that I had lost my fish, but I didn't know what had happened. Everett saw it all and he asked me later if I had seen it. Later the captain apologized and he really felt like a chump for making such a mistake. It really wasn't all that important. We all had a great time and the big fish got away. The world continued to get bigger, but it seemed the more I saw, the smaller it got.

A few years ago, Alberta and I had the great pleasure of going to Mexico with Larry and Shirley. Shirley was exceptionally good at planning trips and finding what to see. She found quite a lot of information about the trees where the Monarch butterflies went. The trip seemed to be rather rough. The kids were not sure about what we could do. They thought that we were about to reach retirement age.

The Monarch's trees are at about 7,000 feet altitude in the mountains. If they were in the United States, there would be tourist accessibility. There is accessibility in Mexico if you really want to see butterflies. We had to take a six passenger plane from Zihuatanejo to a very small airport. There they had an eighteen passenger airplane which we took to Morelia. Alberta had to duck when she got in the plane, the ceiling was so low. We decided that it had been built for very small people. We took that plane to within about twelve miles of the trees. When we got off that plane, we had to take a van for the trip the rest of the way. It was just a one lane dirt road. They had turn-outs about every two miles. If you met another vehicle, between these turn-offs, one had to back up.

We finally got to the taking off place. There was a small log house (office), where you paid $7 apiece. There were no tickets. We just started walking. It was about a half mile to where the trails started. That half mile was quite a climb at 7,000 feet! Alberta ran out of go power about halfway up. Luckily, the management had saddle horses at the office, so we got one and Alberta pushed the right button the rest of the way to where the trails divided. A short trail went up for about two blocks to several butterfly trees. It was a steep climb. Of course, Alberta and I had about all of the climbing we wanted by that time. We took the short trail. Larry and Shirley decided that they would take the long trail where there were more trees. When Alberta and I got to the trees, it was a sight that we couldn't believe. The trees were spruce and about forty feet tall. The butterflies were so thick that you couldn't see enough foliage to tell what kind of a tree it was.

When Larry and Shirley got back, they said that it was a good thing that we did not take the long trail. They thought that it was really not worth seeing.

The big detriment to the development of the sight for tourists was the lumbering business. The land belonged to an Indian tribe. They had been making their living by working for loggers. Some people wanted the tourists and some didn't. We were real glad that Shirley felt that it would be worth working for the opportunity to see the butterflies. It sure brought up a lot of questions for me…the big one…How could the butterflies tell which tree?

The answer could be the difference between people and butterflies. We needed a map, some money, five airplanes, two cars, a horse and some good legs to get to those trees. The butterflies only needed two wings, a built in compass, and a tail wind.

We had travelled almost the whole continent, from the east coast to the west coast, from the lakes of Canada to the butterflies of Mexico. Where would we go from there?

We belonged to the Canyon Lake Methodist Church in Rapid. There was a retired minister in the church, Jack Leach, who was going to take a tour group to Israel. It sure sounded interesting, but what a challenge that would be. We decided to go. Jack had studied in Israel and he and his wife Edna had taken several groups over there. While Jack was with the Dakota Wesleyan College in Mitchell a student from Israel had stayed with them. He had gone back to Israel and had started a school there.

In that next spring, Edna was in a severe car accident which almost killed her. She was slow in recovering so the trip had to be postponed until the next year in July.

That summer our son Larry, his wife Shirley, and their sons David and Michael, and our son Glen, his wife, and daughter, Carlin, flew to Florida for a week. We spent the week with them. After enjoying Disney World, Alberta and I flew to New York in a good sized plane.

We had never been on a subway, so we took a subway ride. Then we got together with the tour group and went to get on our plane. I could not have imagined the size of that plane! I felt like I was dreaming.

Me, that little Montana boy, waiting to get on that great big plane to fly across that big ocean and walk where Jesus walked. It was a great trip! We stopped in Ireland to refuel. Then we flew to Athens, Greece where we did the tourist thing. Then we flew to Amman, Jordan. From Amman we took a bus across the Jordan River. What was amazing to

Tourist group with Michael (UK t-shirt)

us was that they took our passports and just gave us a piece of paper to show that we had been in Israel. When we left they took it back. We have nothing to show that we were ever in Israel.

Israel was certainly an eye opener. A large percent of the people in the United States have no idea what the people over there live on. We waste more in one day than they live on for some time. There was no trash of any kind. There was not a gum wrapper, a cigarette butt or scrap of paper anywhere. The donkeys come down the street bringing things to market. There is someone around to pick up the droppings to put on their garden.

I always thought there was a lot of sand, but there are rolling hills and a lot of rocks. The rocks are from marble size to twenty pounds or over. They are all over the hills. The Jordan River Valley is about 60 miles long and 25 miles wide. The weather never gets below 40 degrees. They can raise several crops of alfalfa. The land in the valley is so valuable that the only animals raised in the valley are milk cows. The feed is trucked out for chickens, turkeys, goats, and sheep. There are no beef cattle or pigs.

Almost all the cars are small and there are about five taxis to every car. There are very few stop signs. There are stop lights down town. The cars miss one another by inches as they go through cross streets. I asked a clerk, who had been to the United States, how they could drive the way they did. He said that a six inch miss is as good as ten feet. He also asked how much gas was burned at a stop sign. With gas at $2.25 a gallon, I would miss a stop sign, too. I never saw anyone come to a fast stop. Very, very cautious drivers knew what was expected of them.

At the time we were there, there was quite a bit of tension, but they really went out of their way to protect the American tourist. They were after the American "dolla". They didn't stamp our passports when we went from Jordan to Israel. They just gave us a piece of paper, which they took back when we left. I guess that it was just politics. I'm glad that it wasn't politics with a gun or an invitation to stay longer.

I really learned to appreciate olives. The olive tree never dies, I guess. They just keep on coming up from the roots. The olive is the life blood of Israel. They sell all kinds of olives and olive oil. They cut out the dead wood and make all kinds of fine knickknacks. They are very beautiful.

They still use camels and donkeys. We were at the spring where Moses hit the rock to get water. It is a beautiful, flowing spring and furnishes water for many people. The kids bring their donkeys with three or four large cans anchored on each side to haul water. Tourists aren't supposed to give any money to beggars. Mostly people don't expect it and it is frowned upon. I couldn't resist the temptation. I had collected a handful of change from all over I pulled it out of my pocket and was surrounded. They started yelling, "White money! White money!" The change disappeared in a hurry. If the people weren't as tough and as frugal as the donkey, they would starve to death.

Israel is like lots of other small countries that have more people than they can support. They have to import wood, beads, feathers and then make all kinds of tourist junk along with some fine cloth, shoes, purses, etc. They are great sales people and start very young. You didn't dare carry a package or a purse. If you did, you sure needed something else and whatever they had was the best and you just couldn't get along without it.

That was our initiation into traveling with a tour. We didn't feel too safe, but they liked the U.S. money and they treated us well. It was really fantastic to see the old buildings and to realize that this was the foundation of the Christian religion. It was sure a long jump for one little boy standing on the Wyoming border.

As I live through my 90's, I am rediscovering how fragile and dangerous the world is becoming. I have been knocked out by falling off a horse. I got knocked out playing football. But the semi-consciousness of having a stroke was entirely different.

Having a stroke is, in a way, like being knocked unconscious. I didn't know when it happened. I was taken by ambulance to the Emergency Room. I knew that Alberta was there and a doctor, but I didn't know what was going on. The doctor decided that I should be admitted to the hospital. This happened about 9:00 in the morning. They did not have a room available until about 4:00 in the afternoon. The stroke was quite severe, but it was caught early, and with what doctors know about strokes, they did a super job. I was half asleep much of the time. I was in the hospital about four days when I heard somebody discussing whether I should go to the Rehabilitation Center. I didn't know what or where that was. They had just dismissed a patient, so it was just a few minutes until I had a place to land.

From the start, I was somewhat of a puzzle to the staff. I wasn't used to having someone tell me that I couldn't do things for myself. I really didn't realize how hard it would be to do what I was used to doing. My right foot didn't go where I told it to go. Everyone was really great. They were all very kind and anxious to make things as nice as they could under the circumstances.

I guess that I got a little extra care because I was aware that the exercises would make me better and I was willing to really work at them. Some of the patients thought that some of the things they asked us to do were unnecessary. Of course, having nice lady instructors didn't hurt too much.

The big difference between a stroke and being knocked unconscious was that I had nothing to do with the stroke. I sort of helped the being knocked unconscious. At least I put myself in situations where things could go wrong. The amazing thing is how many times we are living on the edge, and by some chance we survive.

Recently we went to visit our son and his wife in Denver. They live forty miles from the airport clear across Denver. We stayed there for a week. Our son took us to the airport for our return trip home. It had started to rain a little bit before we got there. The Denver airport is quite a bit to contend with in the best of times. Larry checked in our luggage and us; got us wheel chairs, and went home. We were then taken to the proper gate and deposited to wait for our flight. By that time, the storm had become severe. There was a lot of lightning. They do not fly planes under those conditions, so they kept delaying airplanes and finally just closed the airport.

Fortunately, we had ordered wheel chairs. There were two men who came with them. They were wonderful. They tried to get us settled

down before they left. It was still storming. We didn't want Larry to come all that way back for us. The two gentlemen decided to do what they could for us. We thought that we would get a room in a hotel. We told our helpers that we sure needed our bags, which had been checked for Rapid City. They took us to the baggage claim, where a very nice lady tried to help us. She said that even if she got the bags, the airport no longer took them to the hotel. She said that she would make an exception for us. However, we did not get the bags until we got home.

Our wheel chair operators took us to the phones. They did not work well, so they took us to another place. They made the calls, then handed Alberta the phone. Never having been stranded in an airport, and not believing in credit cards, we found that we were slightly low on cash. That sure brought back the old days! The first hotel which we contacted wouldn't take a personal check. The second one, "the port in a storm" did. The men with the wheel chairs stayed with us until we got on the bus going to the hotel.

The lady at the baggage claim had given us a number to try for a flight on Thursday. Alberta called them, had great trouble hearing them, but thought that we had a reservation for 7:45 Thursday morning. We wanted to get to the airport early enough to get on that flight. We got there at 6:30, but could get no help for getting wheel chairs or signing in. We ended up missing that plane.

We finally got wheel chairs and got up to the proper gate. By this time we were wondering if we were going to have to call Larry back in spite of the rain, hail, and Denver traffic. We thought the airport might have a couple of boarders until summer!

At last we got a reservation on a plane. We were taken in our wheel chairs right to the plane. We got on and asked where we should sit. The stewardess said that we could sit anywhere there was a vacant seat. There were no seats and three of us had to get off again.

Through a lot of effort we finally got on a plane for Rapid City. We sure found out one thing; you don't know it all when you are eighteen or one hundred…but, God willing, we continue to learn.

THE FINAL CHAPTER

By

Steven A. Hand

GRANDMA AND GRAMPS MOVED from the home where she was born to the second floor of a retirement facility at the edge of Rapid City in 2004. This facility is set up so that no matter how their health was, they would be guaranteed an apartment or a room until they both died. As needed, health care workers, usually nurses, were available to provide care. As the need rose, the care went right along with it. The facility takes residents to the grocery, plays, concerts, and even the mall. If there are enough people who want to go somewhere, the facility provides a van and everyone just hops on. If there is a medical emergency, there is an ambulance right there to take them to the hospital. They were able to get a one bedroom apartment at the end of one of the wings on the second floor. They had a beautiful view of the valley behind them. Here is their last Christmas letter before they moved out of the house . . .

Dear Friends and Family.

It is time for us to bring you all up to date on what is going on in our lives. I have lived in the same house for eighty out of my ninety years. Sherman has lived there since nineteen forty eight.

We finally decided that it was time for a change. We have been quite well, just losing the strength which we had. and a lot of our energy. Sherman will be ninety two in a few days. He is doing great, but he wants to do just what he used to do. It just does not work. So, we decided to begin a whole new life style. We decided to move into a Good Samaritan Senior Housing Community. It is within a mile or two of our house. It is on a hill and has a fantastic view of its surroundings.

We rented a one bedroom apartment and started moving out of the house. I wish that I could give you a good picture of that, but you would not believe it anyway. We did not realize it at first, but Sherman had to give up everything which was connected with his world of work, where I had only to down-size the household things. He decided to give his boat and pick-up (both of which he loved) to our grandson, Steven. He started putting price tags on everything in our basement. What decisions and what a job. How do you place a value on all of the things out of your past?

Our two boys came home and we got to spend a few days together, with no one else around. Actually this was a rare thing in our entire lives. Then Glen's two boys came. At that time the four of them realized that if they wanted any mementoes, they had to take them then. They did not need more things in their own houses, but each picked out some small items. (Steven wanted to put the house on the truck and take it back with him.)

I started taking things out of drawers and closets. We filled two boxes with enough to make them easy to carry, took them to the apartment and put them away. They were not necessarily in their permanent place, but were out of sight. This went on for a couple of months. Then, some wonderful church people decided that we needed help. They moved up the time for the yard sale and went to work. The men carried the stuff out of the basement. Sherman had a hard time rescuing a few things, which he put in his outdoor shed. The ladies sorted everything. They had pages of price stickers. Even the smallest things got a sticker. The furniture was placed together so that the auction people could pick them up. When the furniture was gone, the men brought large tables. On the next day, very early, the tables were carried into the yard and everything was taken out of the house and placed for the sale. The sale went on for two days. We got to watch, but not help. At the end of the second day, the same helpers gathered up everything that was left, put it in their pick-ups and took it to the church. Part of that will go in the church sale. The only thing left for us to do was to get rid of the refrigerator and stove. They advertised them for us and we got them sold. Our sons will sell the house.

—Love, Sherman & Alberta

Many times they would go for a walk around the facility and come across turkeys or pheasant coming down from the hill. Deer would stop on the lawn and take a nibble or two as they headed their way down to the valley. In the beginning, Grandma would fix meals in the apartment, but it soon became evident that grocery shopping and preparing a meal was more than they could handle, so they began taking their meals in the facility's dining room. They had assigned places and soon became very acquainted with many of the residents and were able to share many stories during meal times.

After Gramps' stroke, it was decided that they should move to the next step where their caregivers were a little more involved. They moved to the first floor and over to another wing of the facility in 2009. The nurse came to visit every day to help with oxygen bottles and basic medical cares. They no longer needed to worry about the stairs, the dining room was closer, and the medical staff was just around the corner. That winter was rather tough on them both. Gramps seemed to get tired more and more and Grandma was having medical issues as well. The spring came and it appeared that their health was coming back. Grandma was doing fine, but Gramps was sleeping more and more. Then, on June 7, 2010, just short of his 98th birthday, Sherman Glen Hand died quietly in his sleep. He went out the way he lived most of his life . . . quietly, patiently, and with a smile on his face. Grandma died two years later after being moved to Denver to be closer to family.

On display at his funeral were his boots, his hat, and his spurs. Resting, like they were ready for him to pick up and head out to check the cows. Everyone showed up to pay their respects. There were people from their church, close friends, people from his story writing class, Toastmasters, old cowboys, and even a fellow who said he worked with him on the highway and saw his notice in the paper. The facility

where they lived sent a whole bus full of people which showed how he affected people even in his last days. But that was the kind of impact he had on people. I decided then that I would write a closing chapter for his book. As I was putting this book together to first get published, it never really seemed to be finished to me. It seemed that the real story behind all his stories were the people who were affected by him. Names long forgotten and since outlived, there really wasn't anyone left to talk to about "the old days". But, I still felt I needed to add a final chapter to the book.

How do you put a finishing chapter onto a life that was so fulfilling, both for the man and the people he knew? Gramps had wild horse rides, late night adventures across country, and quiet times alone. He had been to Washington D.C. and worked in the nation's capital. He had blazed trails in the hills that tourists now use for sightseeing and summer vacations. He went to the holy land of Israel and Jordan and visited the wailing wall of Jerusalem. How can one put a finishing touch to that? It has taken me two years to figure a way to say how he impacted me and those closest to him. Since he finished his story, I thought I should finish mine. Now that I have had the time to reflect and the time to sit and write, I begin.

As I write this last chapter to his book, I'm sitting in Afghanistan teaching some Afghans how to teach themselves. I look around and realize how much Grandpa would have enjoyed this country. He had visited the Middle East, so I think he would have understood what it is like here. I was able to talk to him from Iraq a couple years ago and I tried to describe what the country was like there. His response was a slow and thoughtful, "Well . . . that's just fine." My grandmother on the other hand was very worried that I was in the wrong place! But, that was who he was, day in and day out, calm, cool, and didn't really fuss about much of anything. That is the way I see Afghanistan now. Once you take the violence and the fact that it is a war zone out of the picture, the real people of this country are very similar to Gramps. They are making do with what they have and are glad to have it. I am asked every day I am with the Afghans, what I think of the people and the Taliban and if I'm afraid to be in Afghanistan. My response is probably the same as what Gramps would say, "It's the selfish people that ruin a country. As for my stay in Afghanistan, well . . . that's just fine."

On my last visit with my grandparents, Gramps asked me if I wore boots. I told him that I haven't worn cowboy boots for quite a while and that I could never find a pair that would fit right. He walked over to his closet and dug around in a box for a couple minutes and came back with the last pair of boots he ever bought. He only wore them in the end, to church, so they were pretty much new. They looked new anyway. After closer inspection, I realized that there was a hole wearing in the bottom of each of the soles. He hadn't gotten around to resoling them, but "they hadn't given him any problems", so he figured it could wait. It turns out, I'm the only person in our family who has feet small enough to fit his boots. I take them out about every month and wear them for the day. Somehow I feel a little taller with them on. I wear them when I ride my motorcycle. With his boots and my chaps, I feel like a modern day cowboy riding off in the sunset.

I think about his last days and our last visit quite often. When I first arrived at their apartment, I took one look at him and it took my breath away. I'm not quite sure what happened, but the story I understood was that he had hit his head in the bathroom. There was no real damage, but he had quite the bump above his eyebrow and his eye was almost swollen shut. He looked something like the elephant man. "It doesn't hurt any more, but it sure doesn't look very good!" was about all he said about the mishap. He kept ice on it, took some medicine the doctor gave him, and by the end of my stay, he was almost back to normal.

We would get up about eight or nine, have a bowl of cereal, and play cards. It was usually Cribbage, or if Grandma was up to it, we would play Pinochle. We would play until lunchtime. Grandma would say, "Come on Sherman, put that stuff away, it's time to go to lunch!" He would turn to me with that glint in his eye, "I 'spect we better do what she says!". We would pack up the cards and Grandma would take my arm and we would start down the 50 yards to the dining room. Gramps would take off with his walker. "Sherman! Slow down!" would come the call from about five yards behind him. He would reach a bench about midway down the hall and he would sit down to catch his breath, but really he was, "just waitin' for you". We would finally arrive and Grandma would sit next to him for about five minutes and he would start off again. At the entrance to the dining room, there was an overstuffed chair. This was his second stop. Again, he would wait for Grandma and me to catch up, and then he would head over to our table. "There! We made it!" was always his proclamation upon reaching the table. It was as if he never really knew if he could make it. I never had the feeling that he couldn't.

The little race took me back to two years earlier. I just finished this book and wanted to visit before I left for Iraq. They lived on the second floor of the complex and we were going to take a car ride around the Black Hills. When we got to the top of the stairs, he handed me his walker and headed down the long staircase. There wasn't even any hesitation . . . until Grandma saw him! "SHERMAN HAND! WHAT ARE YOU DOING!" "We're just going to the car. You don't need to worry about me." "Well, I do worry about you and you know better than to not take the elevator!" I think she was about to have a heart attack, imagining him falling down the long staircase to the door. But he always seemed to know just what to say, "I'm sorry, I won't do it again." He gave her that little grin of his and she melted back to herself, but she had to add, "Well just make sure you don't."

After lunch we would make the trek back to the room, Grandma on my arm and Gramps blazing the trail. He would skip the overstuffed chair and drive straight to the midway bench. Again, he would stop and wait for us to catch up. After a bit, "well Grandma, you ready to go?" He would pat her on the leg and start the final leg of our short journey. We would reach the apartment and he would make his way to the couch that they brought from the old house. The couch was too low for them now, so in typical Gramps fashion, the couch needed to be "fixed". Boards were arranged under the legs to give a little extra height. "That'll work just fine!" he said with a confident sense of accomplishment. His shoes were usually too tight on his feet, so once he got back to the couch, he would change into his slippers. He would then sit back, take a deep breath, and almost within seconds, would be asleep.

When our naps were over, we would gather at the table for another game of cards or we would play dominos. Gramps and me . . . head to head . . . with poor Grandma looking on, "just look at you two boys!" The banter back and forth with exciting moves and attacks . . . we were at war! Grandma slipped in the occasional surprise play with a short little giggle from her. By the end of the game, it was time for supper and the race to the dining room. Gramps worked his way back to the couch to change out of his slippers and put on his "running" shoes. I gathered the cards and Grandma wiped off the table. When everyone was ready, she again took my arm and he took off down the hall.

At supper, they always liked to have their "pearl tea". Grandma's mom made it for her and it became a ritual at supper. A half a cup of hot water to a half a cup of milk. Grandma added some artificial sweetener, but Gramps had to have the real thing, so he put two packets of sugar in his. After supper, Gramps would sit back and kind of pat his stomach, "That was just right!" We all got up and the race to the bench was on.

Just before bedtime, the nurse came in and checked his oxygen and made sure all was right before they climbed into bed. I made my bed on the couch and we talked a little before they dosed off to sleep. I thought of the many nights as a child, we would make our beds out in the living room of the old house. Grandma would bring out the bedding and Gramps would get the thin mattress pads from the basement and we would sing songs and tell of the adventures of the day. During the summer, Grandma would pay us a dime for every book we would read. We would go to the library once a week and get books for the week to read. At night we would lie on our backs and tell of the book we read that day. We would almost always end up singing She'll Be Coming 'Round the Mountain just before we fell off to sleep.

We would use those same mattresses at the ranch on the old faux leather couch that you could turn into a bed by raising up the seat until you heard the click, click, click, then pulled it out and down. I always seemed to hit my head on the wagon wheel armrests of the couch. We would take the same pads out on the porch of Melgrin's cabin and zip ourselves into our sleeping bags and watch the stars. And sure enough the song would come flowing out, first one voice, then pretty soon everyone was singing. We would all fade off to the chirping of the crickets.

Now there is no singing, no chirping crickets, only the hissing sound of Gramps' oxygen pump. But still, I was there, and we were together again, if only for a short time, singing myself to sleep. Good night Gramps. I'll see you soon.

Sherman Glen Hand—June 30, 1912—June 7, 2010